Haunted by Waters

Haunted by Waters

The Future of Memory and the Red River Flood of 1997

**Edited by
David Haeselin**

The Digital Press at the University of North Dakota
Grand Forks, ND

Creative Commons License
This work is licensed under a
Creative Commons
By Attribution
4.0 International License.

2017 The Digital Press @ The University of North Dakota
Beta 0.2

ISBN-13: 978-0692882573 (Digital Press at The University of North Dakota, The)

ISBN-10: 069288257X

Library of Congress Control Number: 2017907324
Digital Press at The University of North Dakota, The, Grand Forks, ND

Cover Image: Flood in 1897. DeMers Ave in East Grand Forks. Taken at the foot of DeMers Bridge. OGL #242, Box 52. Elwyn B. Robinson Department of Special Collections, Chester Fritz Library, University of North Dakota, Grand Forks.

Eventually, all things merge into one, and a river runs through it. The river was cut by the world's great flood and runs over rocks from the basement of time. On some of the rocks are timeless raindrops. Under the rocks are the words, and some of the words are theirs.

    I am haunted by waters.

    Norman Maclean, *A River Runs Through it*

Lake Agassiz, the Pleistocene glacial lake that formed the valley, had returned, a ghost haunting from the past.

    Jane Varley, *Flood Stage and Rising*

Haunted by Waters:
The Future of Memory and the
1997 Red River Flood

Preface: The Flood
Mayor Michael Brown vii

1. The Flood Today

What Does the Flood Mean Twenty Years Later?
David Haeselin 1

We Survived the Red River Flood:
A Tour of the Red River Valley Today
The Student Editors 5

Document: Blue Moose Timeline of the Flood 13

Winter's Labyrinth
Janet Rex 17

What the Voices are Saying
Eliot Glassheim 19

Foreword from Voices of the Flood
Laurel Reuter 25

Conversation with Rex Sorgatz:
Firsthand of the Fire
Kitty Maidenberg...29

911 Call: The Water is Coming 41

2. The Long Process of Recovery

Post Flood Fight
Janet Rex..45

Reflections on Recovery and Tomorrow
Lynn Stauss 47

A Conversation with Lynn Strauss:
We were Finished with Recovery 10 Years Ago
David Haeselin 49

Sharks in my Basement?
Lee Murdock 53

A Pint of Summer
Kent Bergene 61

A Conversation with Ken Vein:
I'm Glad that you Don't Associate
Grand Forks with the Flood!
Michala Prigge 63

911 Call: FEMA 73

3. Building for the Future: Infrastructure Post Recovery

Document: The Red River Greenway 79

Habitat Home
Janet Rex 93

Document: Re-imagining Downtown. 1997 99

Undercurrents: Water Politics in the Red River Valley
Sherry O'Donnell 101

911 Call: Women with No Car 109

4. Town & Gown: The University during and After Crisis

Document: University Timeline Draft 113

Document: Flood Gauge Readings 123

Document: Books Lost in the Flood 133

Behind the Scenes at the University
Kendall Baker, Bruce Gjovic, Randy Newman 151

The Unfolding
Janet Rex 159

It Was Like Nothing Else in My Life Up to Now
Josh Roiland 167

A Conversation with Professor Gordon Iseminger
A Fight for History
David Haeselin 183

911 Call: We are Officially Closed..189

5. Lessons

Document: Floods Do Happen! 193

Document: Grand Forks Flood Disaster and Recovery......203

Actions and Activities of the Regional Weather Information Center During the Historic Flood of 1997
Leon F. Osborne Jr. 227

Studying Women in the Grand Forks Flood:
A Sociologist Looks Back Twenty Years Later
Alice Fothergill..235

A Conversation with Eliot Glassheim
The Need for Self-Expression
David Haeselin 239

'97 Flood: Epic or Episode?
Mike Jacobs..245

911 Call: Offer Our Home...251

Suggestions for Further Reading 255
Contributors 257
Acknowledgements 265

Figures

Grand Forks Official Map ix
This was Home, Sweet Home 37
Anheuser Bush Drinking Water Can, 1997 39
Highway Department Offices 59
FEMA Show me the Money 71
Final Draft of Proposed Structure of the Greenway 77
Levee Alignments:
Northridge Hills Courts Option of Floodwall 91
402 Chestnut 97
Libraries Lost 135

Preface
The Flood

Mayor Michael Brown

The Flood. Two words is all that is needed to elicit memories and emotions in those who lived in the Grand Forks area in 1997. It was a turning point in our history and still today affects how we feel about the community, how decisions are made, and how the city looks to the future.

Our feelings about "The Flood" and subsequent recovery are personal, unique. My story includes throwing sandbags with strangers, holding neighborhood feasts on food being lost to powerless refrigerators, being forced from my home twice – once by the river and once by the flood wall – and eventually seeking to recover normalcy, albeit a "new normal."

My story also includes a part of my life I never imagined: Service as Mayor of Grand Forks in nearly twenty years of inspired and inspiring recovery.

Just as these stories are unique, they are also part of a collective. There are thousands of stories like mine and woven together they form a composite of our memory.

Just as importantly, this collection shows us how these recollections and stories, our historical memory, help shape our sense of local identity. A downtown pizza shop is not just a pizza shop, but the seed of a new community blossoming from within the skeleton of a building whose prior inhabitants were evacuated by flood waters.

This book also reflects the very value of being the "Proud Home of UND." Its liberal arts mission encourages young citizens to find meaningful ways to engage with and have real impact on the community – and the world. I am struck by how these student editors have created a space where readers are invited into the type of thoughtful, respectful discussion that is so important, and so rare, in today's society.

The thousands of new residents (university students, university professionals, Air Force families and others) who have come here in the last two decades have no direct memory or personal story of the flood and recovery. That can cause feelings of separation. This book helps us bridge the gap by welcoming all to share in the experience and try to understand it.

Because if the last twenty years has taught us anything, it's that anyone willing to throw a sandbag, muck out a basement, rebuild a front porch, start or restart a business, listen to their neighbors' stories, or otherwise invest their physical and creative energies into this wonderful community belongs here. That person is "one of us."

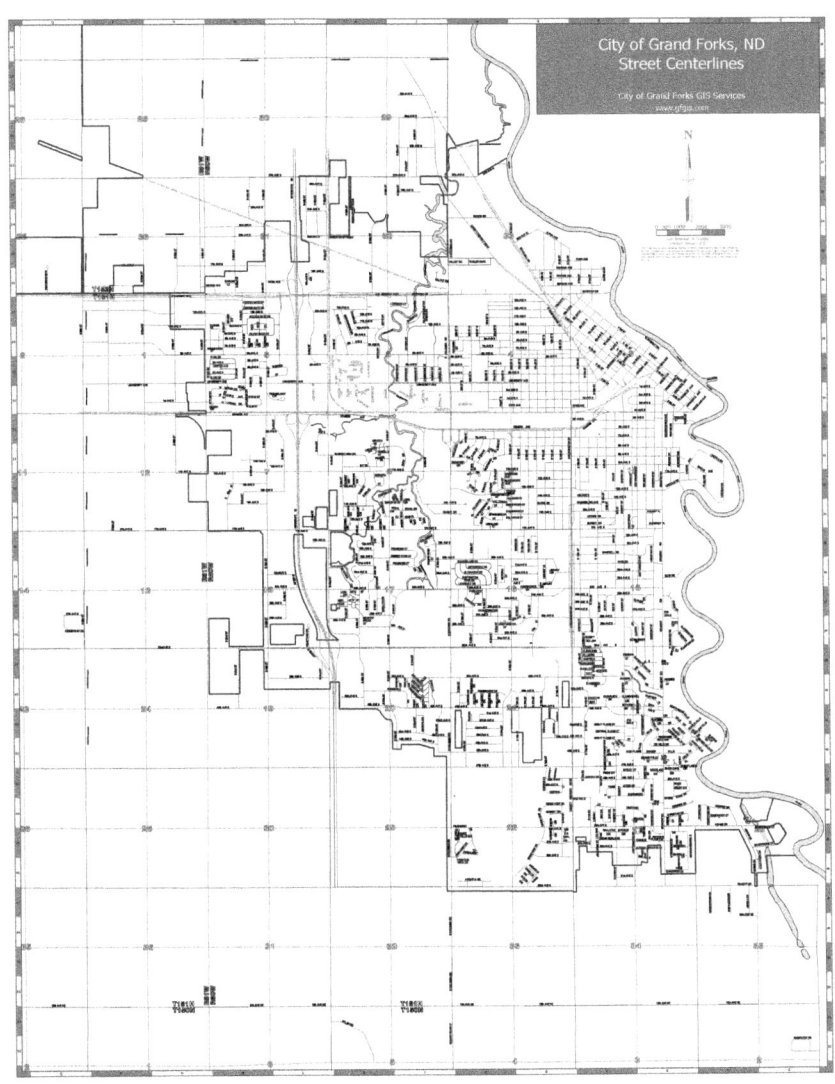

Map of Grand Forks, North Dakota

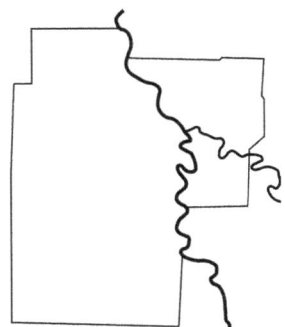

What Does the Flood of 1997 Mean Twenty Years Later?

David Haeselin

Before moving to Grand Forks in the summer of 2014, I did my best to read up on my new home. Immediately, I found articles about the Red River flood of 1997 and the region's long process of recovery. Walk through downtown today and you can't miss the traces of that history. Some monuments to the flood are majestic. The pillar down by the river off DeMers Avenue shows just how high the water got: 54.35 feet. A sculpture on North Third street shows minimalist figures sailing in a lifeboat, struggling to help others on to it while they all brace themselves against jagged waves. But not all these monuments are structures. The Greenway park system is probably my favorite place in Grand Forks, and it is only there because of the destruction caused by the flood. This parkland is also the city's first line of defense. This reminds us that the newer buildings scattered across downtown are not just a sign of growth. New buildings and small pocket parks are there because other structures are no longer. Each new presence is also an absence.

There's a saying that everybody has their own flood story. When I first got here, no one was telling me any. This is probably because most of my social group is comprised of transplants and newcomers, but I think that there's something else to it, too. The pain is still too deep, too raw, even twenty years later. The people of Red River Valley have moved on.

Maybe this should not surprise us. Grand Forks was the largest evacuation of an American city since the Civil War. Thirteen historic buildings in downtown Grand Forks were destroyed by an electrical fire. Downtown will never look the same again. No lives were lost during the flood, but many families lost everything: their homes, their possessions, even their sense of belonging. After the evacuation, some families decided to never return.

The things that need to be remembered surpass any single person's story. The flooding river peaked five feet higher than the original prediction made by the National Weather Service. The levees held, but they were simply not tall enough to hold back all that water. Despite warnings about historic water levels and even a more accurate prediction by the University of North Dakota Regional Weather Information Center (RWIC), few Grand Forks citizens purchased flood insurance. 12,000 properties were damaged in the city of Grand Forks alone, and many more across the region. Citizens were forced to endure thirteen days without running water, and a full twenty-three days without potable water. Financial damages were estimated at $1.5 billion. Studies tell us that women, low-income people, and the uninsured disproportionally felt these adverse effects. Beyond that, the emotional and social toll cannot be effectively measured. During the recovery, 800 residences had to be destroyed or moved to make the Greenway and the new flood protection system. Over 60,000 tons of debris and refuse that once were the material of people's lives needed to carted off and thrown away.

When I polled my students, I found that a few had lived through it and a few had families who had lived here. But those who hadn't knew very little besides that it had happened and that it was a big deal. I kept asking around. I talked to my neighbors, my colleagues, people at the co-op grocery store downtown. I heard stories of snow piled higher than lilac trees, lost family photos, lost beer brewing equipment, and lost antique furniture. I heard stories of normal people coming together to overcome extraordinary circumstances. I heard stories of despair and darkness and of community and collaboration.

The twentieth anniversary of this event gives a new generation of Grand Forksers and Red River valley citizens the occasion to look backward so that they can look forward. Taking stock of how the city and its people have changed in these last twenty years offers us a new chance to envision the future of Grand Forks and the Red River Valley. What's more, we hope that this book can extend the lessons learned through the recovery to others coping with their own unique disasters.

The book pairs archival materials from the Orin G. Libby Manuscript Collection in the Elwyn B. Robinson Special Collections of the Chester Fritz Library at the University of North Dakota with new contributions from citizens and experts who lived through the flood and the region's recovery. The archival inclusions include government documents, student journalism, blueprints, design plans, and transcribed 911 calls. In pairing new stories with these archival documents, the student editors and I hope to inspire new discussions about how the city got to where it is today, so that more people can join the larger civic conversation about the right steps forward for the city, the state, the region, and our nation.

It is important for me to stress that this book is not intended to be the final word on the flood. Rather, it attempts to carry on the conversation started by many other fine works that were released during the city's recovery, many of which were originally published by the North Dakota Museum of Art. We were lucky to the have the chance to include excerpts of some of these in our book. We have also included an extensive bibliography of these works at the end of our own. We hope, if nothing else, this book redirects the rightful attention to those who came before us.

The book is separated into thematic sections. We hope these primary documents add useful context to the personal and professional perspectives offered by our many contributors. More specifically, the editors have paired relevant primary materials with conversations and contributions to explain and complicate recommendations offered by governmental and academic institutions. Since these editors are all interested in American literature in some way or another, we've also tried to add a literary sensibility to these materials through their organization by highlighting some important points of conflict. The major disagreements we discovered while compiling the book were the value of memory and the price of progress, particularly in the role of the historic downtown and university districts. The book also tries to isolate some lessons contemporary citizens can take from the unique conditions of the Grand Forks recovery, the relationship of the city and the university, and the role of bureaucracy and institutions in small town politics.

My students offered many other interesting avenues of inquiry that, regrettably, we had to omit from the final book because of time and space restraints. For instance, some students suggested that we do more to cover the flood's impact and recovery in the rural region between Grand Forks and Winnipeg, Manitoba. Others suggested we look more into the Air Force Base and the National Guard. But as the book began to take its final shape, we concluded that discussions of recovery, historic preservation, and infrastructural development on the city level were so important that we could not afford to tackle the other important issues this kind of investigation brings up. We sincerely hope that others find a way to do so.

Everyone who lived through flood and the recovery has their own story, even though they may not tell them as often anymore. Maybe they assume that everyone who wants to hear them has already. But Grand Forks has changed a lot since 1997; new people have moved here, many of which don't have any personal or family memories of the flood. As a new resident, I feel that not understanding the meaning of the flood means not understanding our neighbors, our teachers, our colleagues, our friends. Ourselves. Everybody has their flood story, but Grand Forks, and the Red River Valley is still writing the story of its future.

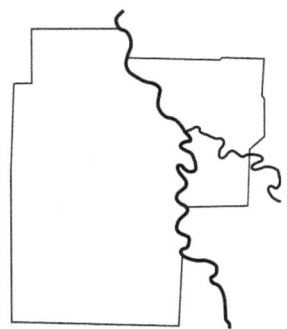

We Survived the Flood: A Tour of Grand Forks Today

The Student Editors

Twenty years after the flood, the city of Grand Forks is vibrant and well, searching for ways to improve and expand. From watery destruction, a community as fierce as the winter winds that wear on it has emerged. North Dakota and Minnesota residents fought to preserve and rebuild after the flood of 1997, but as a newcomer, you'll seldom hear people talking about the spring of 1997. That's just not the Great Plains way.

Signs scattered around the University of North Dakota campus point you towards Downtown, but the main attraction for some of us is a strip of parkland that runs all along the riverside on both sides of the Red. This area is the Greater Grand Forks Greenway, known commonly as the Greenway. Its rolling green hills flow as smoothly as the water they reside by. In the short summer months, the Greenway is true to its name; in autumn, you can see the earth-toned leaves fall into the muddy waters of the Red River. During the winter months, the man-made hills are mountains for kids with sleds, but with spring comes melting snow and the growth of both lush greenery and water levels. During all seasons, you find people strolling, walking their dogs, and, weather permitting, playing Frisbee golf on one of the courses scattered through the system. The Greenway also boasts fifty miles of linked bike trails. This system is known as the "Andy Hampsten Bikeway System." Hampsten, a native son of UND English professors, is a world-famous cyclist known for his skill at climbing steep mountain sides. Given the area's frypan flat landscape, one can't help but appreciate the irony. Hampsten helped teammate Greg LeMond win the 1986 Tour De France, coming in fourth himself.

Comprised of 2,200 acres total, the Greenway also serves as the central part of a 500-year flood protection plan prepared by the US Army Corps of Engineers in the wake of the flood of 1997. This function, however, is often overshadowed by the recreational popularity of the miles of trails and paths along the Red. Each spring when the water creeps up the banks, submerging battered Cottonwood trees near the riverbank, we are reminded of its alternative purpose. The Greenway suggests that from destruction comes growth and the opportunity for improvement, as it has bloomed into a beautiful flower from the remains of cities devastated by the flood.

Walking along the Greenway, you'll come to a spot between downtown Grand Forks and downtown East Grand Forks; there stands the ultimate reminder of the depth these towns have reached in the past 100 years, the highest of them all being the flood of 1997. The flood memorial is just one of many quiet remembrance sthroughout the historic downtown.

If one turns right on DeMers Ave to leave the Greenway, you enter downtown Grand Forks proper. Immediately on the left, you see the Amazing Grains Food Co-op, a staple of the community since 1972, and the best place for vegetarian and other healthy food in the city. On the right, one sees town square. During the summer, the square hosts weekly Farmer's Markets and during the long winter, citizens can ice skate on a frozen pond maintained by the city.

The arts are a central part of Grand Forks culture. From to the annual Alley Alive festival that overtakes the downtown streets to the art walk and street fair, downtown Grand Forks is an important site of self-expression. The main arts hub is the Empire Theatre, located in the heart of downtown on DeMers. The Empire, with its mix of a classic theatre exterior featuring big Hollywood lights and a marquis that hasn't been updated in decades, is a showstopper. Its interior includes modern furniture, clean lines and the art that decorates the walls makes the space feel more like a gallery. The theatre itself is even more eye catching. It features a wide stage, comfortable and spacious chairs, and warm colors to create a dramatic ambiance. Though it was in the midst of a renovation during the flood, the theatre has come back to life with the help of the Grand Forks and regional community. Not only is it a place for the arts, but also somewhere to hold socials, graduation parties, multicultural events, and high school reunions. Even if you are not interested in the arts, the Empire Theatre is a place of gathering and sense of community for all of Grand Forks.

Other places for gathering and sense of community come in the form of dining experiences. Rhombus Guys Pizza is a downtown joint known for its low-key, funky atmosphere. White butcher paper covers every table. Children, teens, young adults, and elderly people all color and doodle on the tables while they wait for their food. T-shirts and beer-related collectibles hang all over the walls. In 2007, ten years after the flood, both Matt Winjum and Arron Hendricks found the small space downtown and decided it was the best place for the unique feel that their business is now known for across the region.

Just down the street from Rhombus Guys Pizza, you will find the recently opened the Rhombus Brewing Company. The brewery is a lively place and, about once an hour, things get even more exciting. Located just feet from the BNSF train tracks, customers seated in the main room get to watch – and feel - the trains rumble by. Legal drinking age college students are often found playing shuffleboard next to business people in the midst of casual meetings, while the smell of boiling wort (the malted barley soup that becomes beer) infuses the air. On an exposed brick wall hangs the 'Uptown Bar' sign next to a historic photo of that bar.

The brewery's building itself is certainly one with its own character, and its own story. Built in 1891, the building began as an opera house before turning into 'Uptown Bar' in 1940. This bar became the trendy place in Grand Forks up to the flood of 1997. The building remained vacant until Winjum and Hendricks decided to install their new brewery in the space. The building is listed as a Historic Preservation site and considered by many to be on the finest architectural examples of the period in the Upper

Midwest. Students, university and Air Force personnel, and thirsty people of all stripes are all glad to be able to gather and drink fine beer in such a fine location.

Another prominent downtown business is the Urban Stampede coffee shop, located just a few doors down on Kittson Avenue from Rhombus Pizza, and around the corner from Rhombus brewing. Local art hangs on the off-white walls; the pressed-tin ceiling, the old booths and tables make up Urban's vintage feel. Sounds of kettles whistling, the churn of foaming milk, typing from business employees or college kids working, and low-key conversations can all be readily heard. Urban has held its rustic vibe since 1992 and through some tragic devastations, such as the flood of 1997. Urban was later rebuilt to reclaim its role as a staple of downtown culture and community.

Nestled in the block between Urban Stampede and Rhombus Guys is Arbor Park, a site of current political controversy. After the flood, the city ended up creating a couple of tiny "pocket parks" in spaces where buildings had to be demolished during the initial stages of recovery. For many in the community, Arbor Park speaks to the need for a creative outlet; it has become a memory of the ruins and a representation of hope for those who remember the devastation that came from the 1997 flood. In the middle of Arbor Park stands the Tree Arbor, a bronze sculpture by Heidi Hoy and Nick Legeros. The park was formed in service of this mission, to speak louder than words about Grand Forks and East Grand Forks' coming together during the spring of 1997.

Within the park, there are metal pieces from buildings otherwise obliterated by the flood and fire, as well as stone and cobblestone from the streets that were used to pave this town. Each piece of art represents what being a community means. The ferocity that community members have exhibited to preserve Arbor Park speaks volumes about the type of people who inhabit this frozen city on the plains. Their warmth, creativity and invigorating passion are palpable throughout the close-knit community.

From art-and-wine walks in the warm July evening, to a cozy HollyDazzle gathering in town square on a cold November night, Grand Forks finds ways to keep their youth, as well as adults, involved. Students are encouraged to participate and get involved throughout the community. Yet, this desire for economic growth and development is as prevalent now as it was after the flood. Many council members believe that by creating more living and retail space there will be an influx of consumerism and diversity in the downtown area, while many citizens are unwilling to lose Arbor Park, a piece of Grand Forks history that makes them feel different and unique. There is a vote scheduled to decide its fate. The future of this memorial hangs in the balance.

Three streets North of DeMers, you come to University Avenue, which runs all the way across town from the Greenway to 42nd Street North and beyond, the site of the city's major growth since the Flood. About halfway up University Ave, you come to UND campus. The university was both affected by and played a big role during the flood fight. Late on April 18, 1997, the Emergency Operation Center (EOC), which handled 911 calls and coordinated public service operations from the fire, police, and EMS, moved from downtown to UND campus. UND remained the headquarters of city operations until long into the initial stages of recovery.

UND affiliated organizations also offered around the clock weather and meteorological updates to Red River Valley citizens and travelers. The Regional Weather Information Center (RWIC), directed and staffed by Professor Leon Osborne, worked around the clock during the flood fight to supply others information. Osborne details this impressive feat of heroic actions from normal people in his contribution to this volume.

Despite UND's relative distance from the river, the flood took a great toll on many buildings on campus. Most buildings were damaged and books from the Chester Fritz Library that couldn't readily be replaced were lost forever in the deluge's wrath. The university was officially closed for an extended period that spring, but was opened for summer classes and with the concept of the "Virtual University." The administration chose to open the campus that summer to move forward in the aftermath of the flood and became instrumental in getting the community back on its waterlogged feet. The law school facilities, for example, served as makeshift offices for the community's law firms as well as courtrooms for legal proceedings.

Today, the university is continually growing, in both adaptations and renovations to campus, as well as number of attending students with each passing year. The students, most of whom live here for a temporary time are as impactful on the community as the flooding, albeit in a positive manner. Though both students' experiences and the flooding are transient, they both brought the community together in a way that is far too rare.

If you turn back towards the Greenway, back to DeMers and cross the Red into MN, just over the Sorlie Bridge, you enter the city of East Grand Forks. East Grand also knows the power of community in the face of the 1997 flood. The waters of the Red ravaged thousands of the city's homes, submerged the bridge, and delivered irreparable damages to the area's local businesses like The Blue Moose and Whitey's. Two decades later, these businesses are lodged comfortably among other enterprises on Restaurant Row, resurrected and revived during the reconstruction process. The East Grand Forks community, with its grandiose city hall building, another symbol of rebirth and recovery, demonstrates what it means to brave the floodwaters and later rise above them. Throughout the city, other buildings such as the Campbell Library or Sacred Heart School, bear witness to the city's recovery after sustained flood damage. Today, whether it's catching a movie at River 15 Cinema, golfing at the local golf course, taking in some of the valley's history at Heritage Village, or grabbing a bite to eat along Restaurant Row, East Grand Forks' commercial operations and downtown appeal greatly diversify the Greater Grand Forks area. For example, the famous Whitey's Wonderbar, decorated with items and news clippings from the Prohibition era, has gone through many changes since its opening in the 1930s . After remodeling and moving three doors down after the flood, Whitey's continues to provide excellent service to its loyal customers with their relaxing atmosphere and famous fried pickles.

It's essential for newcomers to know that Grand Forks and East Grand Forks weren't the only places affected by the flooding of 1997. If you go east on Highway 2, about half an hour, you will find Crookston, Minnesota, home to about 8,000 people in the

Red River Valley and the oldest operating theater in the nation. Red Lake River meanders in lazy loops throughout the town but becomes a cruel enemy in the spring. Red Lake River, which meets the Red River in East Grand Forks, contributed to the extent of the Grand Forks flood of 1997 by adding gushing water and ice jams. The flooding of the Grand Forks area was much worse than Crookston during '97 and, so, the town opened its doors to the fleeing Red River valley residents. Many East Grand Forks residents stayed at the University of Minnesota-Crookston dorms and other university buildings temporarily until they could return home. The town government, motivated by the destruction of Grand Forks and East Grand, has passed measures since 1997 that have improved Crookston's protection, such as building levees and a bypass. Crookston has battled many floods throughout the years, with 2009 being the most recent, and they expect to continue battling the river in the future so Crookston remembers 1997 mostly as a year they could help others.

Driving up Highway 1 and Highway 220 from East Grand Forks, one passes through Oslo, Minnesota, a town of roughly 300 people. Remnants of the flood of 1997 are still noticeable; within the town, there is a wooden light pole with measurements of past floods and the newly built dike as symbolic reminders. Blizzard Hannah and the flood of 1997 severely damaged Oslo. Most people were stranded in their homes and most of these homes were left in ruins after the flood. Nearby farms still flood nearly ever year, and the memories surge back to mind in ways that no dam can hold back. Incidentally, the town just entered the Guinness Book of World Records. In late 2016, a Grand Forks man set the world record for longest float on a pumpkin, riding his massive hollowed up gourd up the Red from downtown East Grand all the way to Olso.

If you go west out of Grand Forks on Highway 2 past the airport, however, you'll eventually reach the northern side of Emerado, where you find the Grand Forks Air Force Base. North Dakota's flat landscape and open sky allows the perfect conditions to have an Air Force base. Today it serves its purpose to react and respond to urgent situations and to provide support, in addition to being a remnant of the Cold War.

At the time of the flood, the Air Force Base had to be used for something else other than aerodynamics-related purposes. Despite the City of Grand Forks' sandbagging for the flood, the Air Force Base had to serve as an emergency relief camp for 50,000 people. During that time, people of different classes and backgrounds had to unite and support each other as they watch their home and city be swept away by the flood. Since then, the Air Force Base still serves its purpose to protect the people and provide support to national security. The base also serves as a major point of contact with UND's Aviation and Aerospace programs. Of particular interest is Unmanned Aerial Vehicle (UAV) research and applications.

Today, twenty years later, we commemorate the strength of the citizens of the Red River Valley as we reflect on the devastation brought on by the natural disaster and cultural upheaval that he now call, simply, the Red River flood of 1997. There is much more to the story than just the flood, though. The rest of the book tries to help build that memory.

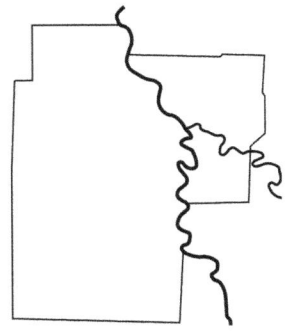

Document:

The Blue Moose Timeline of the Flood

The Blue Moose Restaurant

The iconic Blue Moose restaurant in East Grand Forks offered this timeline of the flood on the front cover of their menu in 1998. These kinds of public documents begin the process of organizing memories of the flood for both visitors and the community.

Reference:
Collection OGL #1351, Box 12, File 5. Elwyn B. Robinson Department of Special Collections, Chester Fritz Library, University of North Dakota, Grand Forks.

We proudly offer the following selections for your dining pleasure/2a

507 2nd St. NW, East Grand Forks, MN
(218) 773-6516

THE BLUE MOOSE
BAR AND GRILL
EAST GRAND FORKS, MINNESOTA

RED RIVER VALLEY FLOOD CHRONOLOGY 1996-1999

November

16-17 — Blizzard Andy dumps 12 inches of snow.

December

16-18 — Blizzard Betty arrives five days before winter officially starts.
20 — Blizzard Christopher, the second blizzard in a week, drops 4.2 inches of snow.
25 — Temperatures plunge to 40 below at Flag Island on Lake of the Woods, setting a record for Minnesota's coldest Christmas.

January

9-11 — Blizzard Doris, wind chills reach 80 below.
11 — The National Guard is activated to clear snow blocked roadways.
12 — President Clinton declares the region a disaster area.
14-16 — Blizzard Elmo arrives, prompting Minnesota Gov. Arne Carlson to close all Minnesota schools.
15 — The U.S. Army Corps of Engineers unveils $40 million ring levee proposal that would protect Grand Forks from a 100-year flood.
22-23 — Blizzard No. 6 is Franzi.

February

14 — The National Weather Service's first outlook on Grand Forks flooding says the river may rise higher than 1979's crest of 48.8 feet.

March

4 — Blizzard Gust adds to the record snowfall, causing the roof of the East Grand Forks Civic Center to sag.
28 — The National Weather Service sticks to its forecast of 47.5-49 feet.

April

3 — Sandbagging and dike building begin in Greater Grand Forks.
4 — Blizzard Hannah arrives with freezing rain that will leave 300,000 valley residents without power. This brings the total snowfall for the year to 98.6 inches.
5 — At Breckenridge, Minn., sandbagging goes on despite the blizzard. Floodwater forces hundreds from the city.
7 — The Red River rises to 38.27 feet. National Weather Service still says 49 feet.
7 — For the second time this year, President Clinton declares North Dakota a disaster area.
8 — Gov. Ed Schafer activates the National Guard to help with flood fighting efforts and blizzard recovery.
10 — East Grand Forks Flood Director Gary Sanders issues a call for 1,000 sandbaggers.
11 — The NWS predicts the Red River will crest during the week of April 20-27.
11 — Dike-walking begins in East Grand Forks.
14 — Red rises to 44.43 feet.
14 — The NWS raises its crest prediction to 50 feet.
14 — The Point Bridge closes in East Grand Forks.
15 — East Grand Forks Mayor Lynn Stauss says 300 to 400 Sherlock Park and Griggs Park residents may have to evacuate by nightfall. The City issues guidelines for evacuation.
15 — Due to ice jams and overland flooding, Warren, Minn., suffers its third flood in less than a year.
16 — The Flood of 1997 officially becomes the Flood of the Century as the river rises above 1979's 48.88 feet.
16 — The NWS changes crest prediction to 50.5 feet.
16 — Grand Forks officials warn residents of possible evacuations.
17 — Red stands at 50.96 feet. NWS raises prediction again to 51.5 feet.
17 — About 1 p.m., hundreds of Lincoln Drive residents evacuate after reports that a nearby dike had broken. The dike is repaired.
17 — East Grand Forks Mayor Lynn Stauss' battle cry of "two feet in two days" urges residents to raise dikes to meet rising crest predictions.
17 — Red River breaks through a clay dike south of Bygland, filling a coulee that passes through East Grand Forks.
17 — The Blue Moose closes at 1 p.m. to allow all employees to sandbag and to hand out sandwiches to the National Guard and other volunteers.

Three Tragic Days: April 18-20

FRIDAY, APRIL 18

2:45 a.m. — Red River at 51.42 feet.
4:15 a.m. — Boils appear in the Lincoln Park dike. City orders evacuation, including 106 residents of Valley Memorial Homes-Almonte Living Center.
6 a.m. — City orders evacuation of Riverside and Central Park areas.
8 a.m. — Water runs out of north end of Lincoln Park Golf Course and down Lincoln Drive.
11:15 a.m. — "It's one of the major disasters of our lifetime," Grand Forks Mayor Pat Owens tells CNN television.
11:35 a.m. — National Weather Service revises its crest projection to 53 feet for today or Saturday.
Noon — River at 52.19.
12:15 p.m. — First break in East Grand Forks dikes comes near Folson Park but ring dike temporarily saves area.
3:30 p.m. — Dike just south of Murray Bridge in East Grand Forks breaks, resulting in the flooding of entire Point area.
4 p.m. — Sirens sound as Point area ordered evacuated, and Murray Bridge closes.
4:30 p.m. — Water in Lincoln Drive area reaches same level as river, leaving about 300 homes in water, many of them to the rooftops.
7:14 p.m. — Red River reaches 52.62, up 18 inches in 18 hours.
8:08 p.m. — NWS revises crest for 54.0 feet on Saturday.
8:20 p.m. — Central Park area fills rapidly.
9:40 p.m. — Emergency Operations Center at Grand Forks police station moves to UND as storm sewer backup runs down Fifth Street. Within 30 minutes, the police station basement is full of water.
10 p.m. — Red River reaches 52.76; Mayor Owens bans sale of alcohol in Grand Forks.
11 p.m. — EGF dike near Kennedy Bridge fails, cutting the last link between the two cities and flooding Sherlock Park homes.

SATURDAY, APRIL 19

Midnight — Water flows off dike by Murray Bridge, flooding land inside Griggs Park in EGF.
1 a.m. — Water comes over the dike by Valley Golf Course in EGF.
2:20 a.m. — Herald pressroom and mailroom employees flee building as sewer backup water rushes down the alley and threatens to overtake downtown.
4 a.m. — Dikes are topped and downtown East Grand Forks - the city's last dry area - is flooded.
5 a.m. — Water is four feet deep in downtown Grand Forks.
6 a.m. — River at 52.89 feet.
7:10 a.m. — Water tops the dike in Riverside Park area.
8 a.m. — Grand Forks water plant fails.
10 a.m. — City orders evacuation of all areas in Grand Forks east of Washington Street.
11 a.m. — UND President Kendall Baker calls off classes for the semester, two weeks before final exams are to start.
Noon — Approximately 50 percent of Grand Forks and virtually all of East Grand Forks are flooded.
2 p.m. — Area east of Columbia Road ordered evacuated.
4:15 p.m. — Fire reported in Security Building, 101 N. Third St.
7 p.m. — Ninety percent of EGF's 8,700 residents have been evacuated.
7:15 p.m. — Planes are dropping chemical retardant on fire.
8 p.m. — Fire has spread to three city blocks.
10 p.m. — Approximately 4,000 EGF evacuees have arrived in Crookston. GFAFB is housing several thousand evacuees.

SUNDAY, APRIL 20

5:30 a.m. — Eleven buildings are either lost or heavily damaged by the fire.
7 a.m. — River at 53.7 feet.
2 p.m. — A helicopter dumps water on the smoldering downtown fire.
7 p.m. — United Hospital evacuates the last of its patients.
8 p.m. — 75 percent of Grand Forks' residents are evacuated.
9 p.m. — River at 53.99 feet.

---

21 — The East Grand Forks Comfort Inn made a home for the city offices of EGF and FEMA.
21 — Red River crests at 54.11 feet.
21 — Classes are canceled for the rest of the year in Grand Forks and East Grand Forks schools.
21 — Emergency Animal Rescue Service sets out in search of pets left behind.
22 — President Clinton tours devastated area via helicopter.
22 — At least 1,500 Pembina and Drayton residents leave homes as dikes crack.
23 — Red River begins to recede.
23 — American Red Cross President Elizabeth Dole tours flood stricken areas with North Dakota first lady Nancy Jones Schafer and Grand Forks Mayor Pat Owens.
24 — Some Grand Forks residents are allowed to visit their homes for a few hours.
26 — Property damage estimated at $775 million in Grand Forks and East Grand Forks.
26 — The first portion of East Grand Forks reopens to residents. Portions of Grand Forks continue to open.
27 — A Northwest Airlines 747 arrives in Grand Forks with 200,000 pounds of flood-relief goods.
27 — Interstate 29 reopens between Grand Forks and Fargo, eliminating a one-hour detour through Casselton, ND.
28 — The Kennedy Bridge reopens after 10 days, uniting Grand Forks and East Grand Forks, and eliminating a three-hour drive between the two cities that are right next to each other.
28 — Dave Homstad, owner of the Blue Moose, enters the restaurant for the first time since April 17th.
29 — An anonymous woman, "Angel," pledges to give $2,000 to every household hurt by floodwaters.

May

1 — FEMA announces it will bring 100 fully equipped trailers for evacuees.
1 — Dedicated employees return to the Blue Moose and start the recovery process.
2 — Nondrinkable water is restored in Grand Forks.
3 — Experts say this wasn't a 500-year flood, but the next flood could be worse, and it could come soon.
4 — North Dakota's Congressional delegation requests an explanation from the National Weather Service and the Army Corps of Engineers on why they didn't share information that might have offered a more accurate flood forecast.
5 — Mayor Owens issues order banning scavengers from picking through debris on the berms.
8 — A second "Angel" gives $5 million for people of Greater Grand Forks.
11 — The Point Bridge reopens.
12 — Drinkable tap water is restored to Grand Forks.
15 — Mayor Owens meets with first lady Hillary Clinton in Washington, D.C.
24 — A National Weather Service team arrives in North Dakota to investigate the flood forecasts.
28 — After 40 days and 40 nights of hard work and dedication from the Blue Mooses employees, the downtown business closest to the river reopens. There was also a brief rain shower on this day that created a vibrant, beautiful rainbow over the Blue Moose on its opening day.

June

9 — The U.S. Army Corps of Engineers proposes three flood-protection plans for Greater Grand Forks.
12 — President Clinton signs revised $8.6 billion disaster-aid bill.

October 4, 1998

The Blue Moose closes so the building can be relocated to the dry side of the dike.

November 13, 1998

The Blue Moose crosses Demers Avenue on its way to its new home!

January 1999

The new Blue Moose reopens at its new location and it's better than ever!!!

Reprinted with the permission of "The Grand Forks Herald"

Ruby on the Red
EGF Centennial Book • The Meeting of the Reds

'Great White Way'

During the 1930s and 1940s, the beer parlors legalized by state law and city ordinance, but still technically illegal in Polk County, quickly expanded their bills of fare to include hard liquor, most of which was smuggled through Canada, and gambling.

The discreet little signs that once adorned storefronts gave way to flashing neon signs, so many that in the late 1930's "Ripley's Believe It or Not" credited a three-block area of East Grand Forks - Demers from the bridge to Fourth Street - with having the highest concentration of neon lights in three-block area of any place in the world.

Hard liquor was smuggled in from Canada, and some may have come from as far away as Chicago. Local tradition has it that such well-known gangsters as Al Capone supplied beer and liquor to East Grand Forks bootleggers.

There were high class bars such as Bobby's Cafe, considered the best steak house west of Chicago. Whitey Larson's Wunderbar and Cafe had the nations first stainless steel horse-shoe-shaped bar and so many slot machines it looked and sounded like a club in Chicago. Kearnes and Waski's boasted a fancy mahogany bar, high-backed booths, and professional gamblers. Kearnes and Waski's was the only place in town with a professionally-run gambling operation offering roulette, blackjack, and high stakes poker.

Because the bars were illegal, the city was deprived of the income normally derived from licenses. To make up for it, the city police staged one or two local raids a year. Guilty bar owners were fined $200 each in Municipal Court, and business continued as usual.

Daily Herald, April 19, 1882

Pure Water

Some soulless miscreant with the conscience of a vitriol thrower, hauled three dead horses into the Red River Monday night or yesterday morning. The river may stand it but the people won't. All of the inhabitants are forced to use Red River water to drink and use in cooking. To have it poisoned in the manner above is execrable. In Fargo, the pollution of the water would be no calamity, there it is only known as the fluid in which glasses are rinsed after the men get together and say "ho!" in concert. But here it is different, and the man who will foully pollute the water is a public poisoner, a wholesale Lucretia Borgia. The police force towed the livestock into the current and started it toward Winnipeg at an eight knot speed. Winnipegers are tough.

BEVERAGES

We proudly offer Pepsi products!

Sodas *(free refills)*	$1.29
Lemonade *(one refill)*	$1.29
Milk *(2%, skim or chocolate)*	$1.29
Large	$1.59
Iced Tea *(free refills)*	$1.29
Raspberry Iced Tea *(free refills)*	$1.29
Hot or Flavored Tea	$.99
Hot Chocolate	$1.29
Juice	$.99
Large	$1.29

OLD FASHIONED ITALIAN SODAS

A refreshing blend of flavored syrups, cream and soda. **$1.59**

Almond	Hazelnut
Caramel	Raspberry
Vanilla	Irish Cream

Also available as an adult beverage:
A Libation Creation

Tell Us Where You Saw the Blue Moose and Win a FREE Dinner For Two

Tell us where you last saw the Blue Moose on the space provided below. Your creative entries will be reviewed weekly for a free dinner for two compliments of the Blue Moose. Please leave your entry with your server or mail it or fax it to us at your convenience.

The Blue Moose was last seen crossing DeMers Avenue. He was moving a little slow but was anxious to get to his new dwelling.

Where did you last see the Blue Moose? _____

_____
_____
_____
_____
_____
_____
_____
_____
_____

Name: _____
Birth Date: _____
Address: _____
City: _____
State/Province: _____
Zip/Postal Code: _____

SEND TO:
BLUE MOOSE
507 2nd St. NW
East Grand Forks, MN 56721
Phone: (218) 773-6516
Fax: (218) 773-3547

COFFEE TIME

We proudly serve only
McGarry Private Estate coffees
in both regular and decaffeinated blends.

Bottomless Cup of Coffee $.99

ESPRESSO

	Single	Double
Espresso	$1.39	$1.89
Cappuccino	$2.09	$2.89
Mocha	$2.89	$3.89
Latte	$2.09	$2.89
Aulait		$2.09
Steamer		$1.89

Flavored syrups are .39 cents.

DAILY FEATURE STORIES

Monday Moose Night
Buy one char-broiled classic burger, get one FREE!

Tuesday – Ole and Lena Night
$7.99
Assorted ribs glazed with our homemade Norwegian BBQ sauce.

Walleye Wednesday
$9.99
A perfect sized walleye portion broiled, pan fried or lemon peppered.

Prime Time Thursday
$10.99
10 oz. of slow roasted prime served with hot au jus. Choice of side.

Friday and Saturday
Ask your server about our special culinary delights created by our talented kitchen crew. While supplies last.

Saturday and Sunday
Come in and check out our new weekend brunch menu. Served table side from 11:00 a.m. to 2:00 p.m. on Saturday. 10:00 a.m. to 2:00 p.m. on Sunday

Bloody Mary Bar
New to the **Blue Moose**!! Experience the best Bloody Mary in town. Why is it the best? Because *you* create it! Six feet of fixins to choose from. Saturday from 11:00 a.m. to 4:00 p.m. and Sunday from 12:00 noon to 4:00 p.m.

JUST DESSERTS

Moose Mud Pie $3.99
A Blue Moose classic! Four layers of ice cream: New York vanilla, chocolate, coffee and toffee piled high into an Oreo crumb crust with whipped cream, hot fudge, carmel and pecans. YUM!!!

Specialty Cheesecake Du Jour $3.59
A monster slice of homemade cheesecake. Ask your server about today's selections.

Chocolate Cherry Velvet Cake $3.49
Moist double chocolate cake loaded with chocolate, hot fudge and cherries topped with whipped cream.

Sundae $3.39
New York vanilla ice cream topped with your choice of Hot Fudge, Carmel, Strawberries, Chocolate or Raspberries. Smothered with whipped cream and cherry on top.

Sorbet $2.19
Pureed fruit, sweetened and frozen. A nice palate cleanser!

Turtle Bread Pudding $3.49
Cubes of French bread folded in a rich custard with spices. Served warm with caramel, fudge and crunchy pecan pieces. Topped with real whipped cream.
A la Mode add $.39

CLASSIFIED SECTION

FOR SALE
Hats
T-shirts
Sweatshirts
Tank Tops
Kids T-shirts
Moose Mugs
& Many Other Items
All these are for sale at The Blue Moose. See your server or bartender for details and prices!

COMING ATTRACTIONS
Live bands on Thursday nights at the Blue Moose starting at 10 p.m. We be jamming until close!

TRUE BLUE BARGAINS
Drinks, appetizers and Happy Hour items. Ask your friendly server or bartender.

MISC. ITEMS
Wine, champagne and specialty drinks that go perfect with every meal.

FOR RENT
UPSTAIRS LOFT FREE with purchase of food and beverages. The Blue Moose is the ideal place for hosting your Business Meetings, Birthday Occasions, Going Away Parties, or any other special events. Please ask your server for details or call (218) 773-6516.

The Blue Moose is the ideal place for hosting your business meetings and get-togethers.

Please ask your server for details or call

(218) 773-6516.

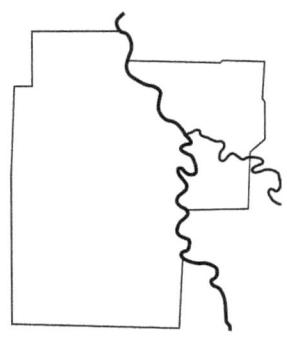

Winter's Labyrinth

Janet Rex

All I touch has turned to snow—
         coneflowers,
cups and saucers, violets. Our Golden's gone

in a craze of snow,
         intricate as
any castle hedge maze. What's he finding?—

too late rabbits, tea
         with Alice, blackbirds
in a pie? I caw for him, my nose

snapped by cold,
         my eyes blind
to this hazy beauty, for my daughter's

frozen to the TV daily,
                while my silver blade's
swinging through the sparkling

powder. Pausing.
                Only two hours
into this brisk shoveling, I scream

into the wind. Stillness.
                Voice. Stillness.
Until there! Echoing back

through a blaze of flurries,
                flashing
on some fresh minted path, the dog

leaps out like fire,
                ears flying
under a dazzling crown of snow.

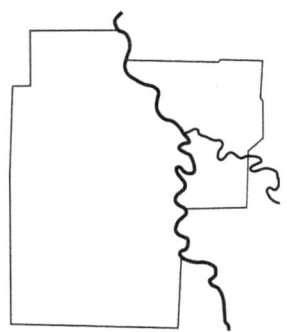

What the Voices Are Saying

Eliot Glassheim

From *Voices From the Flood* (1999)

After the flood, whenever friends or even casual acquaintances ran into each other, the first thing they did was to tell their stories. How bad was the damage, where did they go, what was it like leaving town, what did they take with them, how long were they gone, had they known in advance it was going to flood, how were the children taking it, what about pets, where were they staying now, were they going to rebuild, was the city helping?

But even after they had told their stories many times, people still wanted to tell the next person they met. One had the impression of a city of ancient mariners, "stopping one of three" at a wedding, compelled to tell their haunted stories to purge the experience from their minds. And, for the listeners, at least for the first few months after the flood, we never tired of hearing the stories told over and over again. They were all way of expressing a shared bond, of saying how we were part of the same event, an epic event so large in our lives and so broadly shared that it required telling.

But I also think that telling our stories was a way of reestablishing control. The flood did things to us. destroyed our homes, uprooted us from every normal way of life we had built up over many years, overpowered all our certainties, threw us into exile and wandering. Once we came home, it forced us to face the unpleasant task of cleaning up, throwing out, and starting over. In the course of telling our stories of what the river's overwhelming power had done to us, we found little glimpses, some humorous, some gritty and determined, of what we had done in response. It was a way of remembering who we were. Telling our stories helped us knit ourselves back together, see ourselves again as active makers of our lives instead of suffering victims.

This revelation of the well-spring of storytelling interested me. Instead of looking at stories as merely frills or pleasant diversions, I was struck by the deep need to tell as the bedrock of human psychology upon which poems, epics, plays and novels (and even political speech) are founded. Though of course more formal histories of the flood will be written in the future, it seemed important to me to capture the authentic voice of a variety of people telling their personal flood stories.

Who might be interested in reading these stories? In addition to those who went through the Flood of 1997 in Grand Forks and East Grand Forks, their children, relatives and far-off friends will be interested to know what happened. Certainly those who work with disasters all over the world will be interested to see how people reacted, what they heard and felt no matter what those in authority thought they were doing or saying. And public officials who have to prepare for an assortment of disasters, as well as lead the recovery of their people from devastation, may also be interested in what the stories have to tell them.

But, even though these voices are the stories of sixty individuals talking about a particular flood in a particular place, I think they are likely to be of interest to an even wider audience. These voices from the flood are speaking under the pressure of intensely focused events. As such, the stories they tell seem to have a universal, timeless quality to them. Like a great basketball player taking off near the foul line for what will become a slam dunk, images from these stories hang in mid-air, moving, yet, for those few seconds, motionless.

Some of the images in this book seem fresh to me even after many readings:
- Stranded in a truck surrounded by four or five feet of water, a man lassos a garbage can and telephone pole which were

floating by, lights a fire to keep warm in the early evening, and then signals a helicopter to rescue him from the dark, cold night.
- Not evacuating when the power and water are shut off, a high school senior and his family live in a state of nature for two weeks. He fishes off his back porch, canoes down a main street, visits abandoned houses of friends, and brings home food and generators in the canoe.
- Firemen wake a college senior and hustle him out of his apartment with no time to collect his wits or a novel he's been writing. Because his sense of smell was lost in a recent accident, he has no idea the building next door is burning and no idea, until later, that the firemen have saved his life.
- An elderly couple, who married when each of their spouses died of cancer several years ago, have no time to prepare for grief when they see their home, which had taken water to the rooftop, bulldozed down without warning. The machines run over the trees in their yard which officials had not allowed them to give to their children for transplanting.
- The city sees itself differently because it was the object of national attention. As one person whose parents were interviewed on national television put it, "You'd think that we were in some small place on the earth and then all of a sudden everyone's here and all the things you see on TV are at your house."
- Before the grown children who had come back to help their parents clean leave town, the family gathers at their ruined house with their priest, who performs a formal ceremony to help them find closure. Later they bury a time capsule in the yard, under the evergreen tree they planted twenty-four years ago.
- After evacuating, some people sneak back to their houses, possibly risking their lives to take what is important to them: a wedding ring, some valued art works, one by a long dead relative.

- During the demoralizing mucking-out process, one couple believes they are fighting the effects of the flood by planting flowers.
- If she can't save the piano given to her as a farm girl by her grandfather, one woman is going to plant the brass piece in her yard for morning glories to climb on.
- Shortly after people returned to town, one man saw people running out of $250,000 houses to get Red Cross hot dogs and concluded that "the flood was a great equalizer."

Beyond the images, those interested in human nature can hear in these stories a broad range of raw emotions. Moments of fear, courage, foolhardiness, neighborliness, determination, greed, love of family, stoic acceptance, anger, compassion, blaming, selfishness, generosity, self-pity, grief... they all present themselves directly, unmediated by conscious narrative technique. Most of the classic virtues and deadly sins reveal themselves in these miniatures.

One of the stories I found most astonishing was that of a woman who begins by revealing, to herself and to us, that she wants to leave town because she feels betrayed (by the city? by the river? by life?). In the course of the interview, she engages in an on-going internal dialogue as she reflects on other people's attitudes towards the flood. She reacts to a letter to the editor claiming that God sent the flood in retribution for our sins; she reads the Biblical story of Job; she draws cheer from a miraculous newspaper clipping about a Cherokee Indian prisoner from the east coast who sent his $12 monthly cigarette allotment to help Grand Forks flood victims. He accompanied his gift with a note which said that any Indian knows that you don't put your tipi by the river. In the end, she seems to be almost reconciled to the fact that the water didn't mean to hurt her personally and, as a result, to realize that, as she takes the disaster less personally, she is feeling less betrayed.

I think the experiences in these excerpts from transcribed interviews fairly represent our 1997 flood, though each person was interviewed as an individual rather than as a representative of some demographic group. To the extent that the interviews are representative, what do they say? Certainly each reader will shape the raw material differently. For myself, I am brimming with pride at my fellow human animals for their ability to see both themselves and what happened to them clearly. They may not like it, but they look it straight in the eye and, with some hesitation (whose cadence I have tried to retain while editing the transcripts), they say it straight. They were dumb not to see it coming; they learned a tough lesson; they don't blame the river; they were almost happy to learn that material things are okay but strong relationships are better; they grieve their losses; they're going to rebuild and move forward.

What a sad, proud day it was when thousands of cubic feet of water poured through the streets of Grand Forks and East Grand Forks each second, and tested us all for years to come.

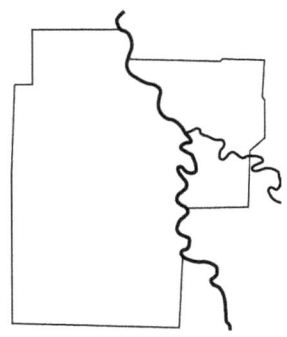

Foreword to *Voices from the Flood*

Laurel Reuter

From *Voices From the Flood* (1999)

I remember. I remember cold and exhaustion. I remember overwhelming cold and bone-deep exhaustion. I remember winter storms banking record snowfalls on frozen, water-saturated land. Ice and snow. Blinding blizzards. Canceled school. Canceled work. Canceled everything. Region-wide power outages. Sandbagging. Broken dikes. Electrical fires born of the icy waters gutting the inner core of the old city. Evacuation. Temporary lives lived in other places. Homecomings followed by months of sorting out in both private and public life.

Two years ago in the early spring, when the Red River turned western Minnesota, eastern North Dakota and southern Manitoba into a vast inland sea, our lives changed forever. Muddy waters, as far as the eye could see, sat upon our land. Floods on flat, inland plains creep in, seemingly stay forever, and then slowly sink away. Time becomes endless. And through all of it, I remember overwhelming cold and bone-deep exhaustion.

The flood dealt a severe blow to the very fabric of civic and cultural life. Churches, our only synagogue, both private and public libraries, cultural institutions and public buildings of all kinds were damaged or destroyed. The region's daily newspaper burned. Several elementary schools, one middle school, numerous daycare centers, and a Catholic high school were condemned to demolition. Neighborhoods were destroyed and businesses crumbled. The powerful and the powerless were hit equally hard.

The North Dakota Museum of Art, situated at fifty-four feet, escaped by inches-even though the river crested at fifty-four feet. Its lift station held, so the water couldn't surge up through the storm sewers as it did all over town. I, the founding director of the Museum, was handed a miracle. My friend, Margery McCanna Jennison, opened her summer farm home for me thirty miles away in McCanna, North Dakota. Her cousins, Ralph and Colette McCanna, fed me. I became a commuter-my own house having been less lucky. Aided by the kindness of friends and families of friends, I was able to take up the real business of a museum.

Years before I had drafted the Museum's Mission Statement. My dosing tenet stated that "the museum would be a place of refuge." I had also written, "We, as inhabitants of the Northern Great Plains, struggle to ensure that the arts are nourished, and that they flourish, because we know that a vital cultural life is deeply essential to isolated people." Only much later would I understand how prescient those words had been. It was clear to me from the beginning what the Museum's role must be. Within days I made the following public announcement:

> May 15, 1997 - The North Dakota Museum of Art is available, free of charge, to the community for religious and ceremonial purposes, including weddings, memorial services, ordinations, or religious services. The Museum also offers its space and assistance to other arts groups, or not-for-profits, needing a place to meet, perform, practice, or regroup. We recognize the fragility of cultural life in times such as these and so offer our services to those who need them.

The Museum became a center of community life. People flocked in for free concerts coupled with community-wide potluck suppers. The burned-out North Dakota Ballet Company held regular practice sessions. Habitat for Humanity took up residence. Special art classes were begun for uprooted and displaced young children. The galleries became a home for the East Grand Forks Bible

Baptist Church-three times a week for over a year. In the midst of endless activity, life began to reconfigure itself.

Days turned into weeks and I found myself relearning larger truths. Life shatters along existing fault lines. Disaster accelerates change. Shaky marriages end. Marginal businesses go under. Farmers sell out and move to town. Nursing homes fill. Whole segments of the business community make generational shifts. Change mandated by nature begins to feel ordinary. Yes, to provide a refuge during turbulent times was important, but other work remained.

We had been homeless, exiled, wanderers. Most of us were not able to return to our homes for over a month. Second only to cleaning out the wreckage was the overwhelming compulsion of everyone we met to tell their story. When did it first dawn on them that the water would win, that nature could not be controlled? When were they evacuated? Where did they go? Who helped them? When they returned what did they find? How high was their water? What did they lose? What happened to their friends? What's in the future? Everyone needed to tell, over and over again, his or her story.

I didn't know much about oral histories, only that this community needed one. I began to call around. Certainly there were specialists who could teach us. I stumbled upon Jaclyn Jeffrey, an oral historian at Baylor University, and she agreed to come to Grand Forks to help us begin. But I needed to find someone in Grand Forks to head up the program. I turned to Eliot Glassheim, a Ph.D. in literature who worked for me at the Museum. He didn't convince easily. Why would a contemporary art museum organize an oral history project? What business was it of ours? Finally he came on board-only to spend the next two years immersed in what was to become a three-part oral history. The stories of ordinary people told in this book came first, to be followed by the stories of the officials, and then the first written history of the Grand Forks flood based on hundreds of interviews with city staff.

Finally, I needed one more member of the team: a historian from Grand Forks who could guide the project after Jaclyn Jeffrey returned to Waco, Texas. We discovered Dr. Kimberly Porter, a historian on the history faculty at the University of North Dakota.

Within three months of the flood an army of volunteers had begun to canvas the community, searching for singular stories that would amalgamate into the collective tale that unfolded on this vast flat valley as it was overrun by powerful waters. This book contains the shards of that collected memory, stored away for future residents of this ancient lake bed that later became known as the Red River Valley. The North Dakota Museum of Art saw to their gathering, to giving them shape and form, and now returns them to the people. Thus histories have always been written.

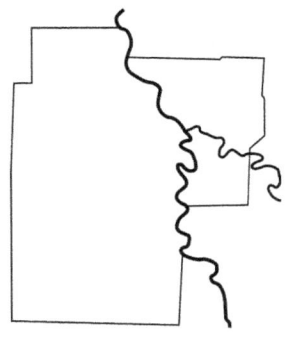

Conversation with Rex Sorgatz

Firsthand of the Fire

Kitty Maidenberg

From *Voices From the Flood* (1999)

As an English major at the University of North Dakota, Rex Sorgatz actively initiated and promoted a variety of musical events, a new mass circulation arts magazine, and improvisational theater prior to the flood. He lived in an apartment fifty feet from the Security Building, where the fire started which burned his building and ten others in downtown Grand Forks. A novel he was writing was lost in the fire. He graduated from the University and, in early 1998, he moved to Minneapolis to work at the Web Guide Monthly. He spoke with Kitty Maidenberg on July 11, 1997 about his dramatic evacuation.

Rex: Friday night I turned on the radio. It was pretty late, about eleven o'clock at night. I called my friend Simon, an English graduate student who lived across the street. I woke him up and I said, "We're in an evacuation zone. Should we leave?" He said, "No, I don't think so. I'm going back to sleep." I said "Okay." So I figured I'd go to sleep too. Then about midnight he calls and he says, "There's water in our street. There's just a little bit of water coming up the curb. Should we leave?" I said, "Well, you know, I don't know. Let's go walk around town." So we went outside and walked over towards where Sanders was, and the Urban Stampede.

At that point the water that had come through town — all the way from the south end up through the Lincoln Drive area — was just coming over the railroad tracks. It was like a waterfall, pouring over the railroad tracks and coming into downtown.

We walked around and got to the police station, which was surrounded by water except for one little inlet. By that time they had to take all the prisoners out over this moat. We started walking back toward our apartment, which was only about four blocks away, and my car was still sitting in the street because there was no water where we were yet. I said I was going to go move my car into the parking ramp. He asked if l was going to leave and I told him I didn't think so. And he said, "I think I'm going to go." So he left and went out to the University. I moved my car over to the parking ramp and I went upstairs and went to sleep.

The next morning I woke up and there was six feet of water on my "front lawn," in my street, and I knew I probably should have left last night. There wasn't much I could do now except call for the Coast Guard but I decided that there was no real necessity for me to get out. I mean, I had had an inclination that this might happen so I'd purchased ten gallons of bottled water.

Kitty: You were in an apartment on the second floor?

Rex: Yes. And I had enough water and enough canned goods to last me for at least a month probably. I had a lot of writing I wanted to do and I had access to a computer. So I really was looking forward to being alone, in solitude, and getting all this stuff done. I decided I would stay and not bother asking the National Guard to come and fetch me out.

That Saturday was really a beautiful day. It was about 75 degrees. It was sunny, really, really sunny. You can climb out my window and you get onto the next building's roof. I decided to climb out there and lay in the sun and read. And, you know, I was watching the National Guard come through on their boats and pick up a blind man across the street. I'm sure he called for them. They shouted up and asked if needed to get out so I said, "Nope, I'm fine." I was laying out there in the sun reading a Toni Morrison novel and I actually had a great time despite watching all this water flow through my downtown.

I was out there most of the afternoon. At four o'clock I went in and I laid down to take a nap, and was woken up at about five o'clock by firemen, banging on the door with the butts of their axes, screaming, "Fire! Get out!" They didn't know that I was in there, they were just going to every door and banging.

Kitty: And actually breaking them in?

Rex: No. At that point they weren't. I was groggy, and I didn't even answer the door right away. They were yelling "Fire!" and I thought it was just their way to scare somebody out. I didn't actually think there was a fire. But I got up, opened up the door, and there was no sign of fire. The firemen had gone on to the next door already. They saw me and they came back and they asked me a couple of questions and said I had to get out right now.

Kitty: Asked you questions to find out if you were okay?

Rex: It had taken me about thirty seconds to answer the door and they thought maybe I wanted to stay so bad I wasn't going to answer the fire call. But I said, "No, I was just sleeping." Then they realized there might be other people in this building, so that's when they started taking axes to all the doors. They started breaking in everyone's doors. Not that it mattered, because the building burned down later.

I was escorted out right away and at this point I'm still not really believing it's a fire. I mean, I didn't not believe it but I just assumed that they were saying that to get people out. About a year ago I lost my sense of smell, so it probably smelled from smoke and fumes when I was leaving but I just didn't know that. I probably would have slept through it all if the firemen hadn't woken me.

So then I was taken outside and as soon as I walked outside all of a sudden it was about 150 degrees and the flames were flying up in the building next door. By that time the fire had jumped from the Security Building next door to the building where Griggs was located and it was just going to start on my building. I walked down the back fire escape and was put into a Coast Guard boat and taken away, passing all along the way fire engines that were in the street.

I asked. the Coast Guard driver why they were there and he said, "Well, they're stuck. They can't get through all this water." About four blocks from my apartment I was put into a National Guard Humvee. They asked me where I wanted to go and I said Hawaii. They said, "Well, we'll take you to the University." So they dropped me off at the Memorial Union at UND and I'm not even up the stairs more than three steps and I ran into Liz Fedor from the Grand Forks Herald. She wanted to interview me. I said, "Sure."

Kitty: When you left your building with the firemen, did you take any books or anything. Did you take the Toni Morrison?

Rex: Here's what I did. I got up, put on my coat, I don't know why, I was still groggy. I put on my coat and I put my backpack on. And when I started walking out I said to the fireman, "I probably don't need my coat, do I?" He looked at me oddly, like he knew that my place was going to be burning down. At the time I didn't know that. I had no idea how serious it was. It could have been somebody's oven on fire or something. And so I took off my coat and I threw it back in the apartment. (Laughter) And he looked at me really strangely. So all I had with me was my backpack. It had five books and a pair of jeans in it. That was all.

Kitty: You didn't take your computer?

Rex: No. No, I didn't. No, I mean, as soon as I walked outside and saw the flames I wanted to go back but they wouldn't let me.

Kitty: So this writing project that you were doing was lost?

Rex: Everything. I lost every piece of writing I ever had. And that's a lot.

Kitty: You spent Saturday night on campus. When did it dawn on you that you didn't own anything anymore?

Rex: Well, we climbed up on top of the roof of the Old Science Building on the UND campus, where the radio station is located. And we were watching the planes dropping the red dust onto the downtown buildings. At that time we really didn't know the extent of the fire. I went downstairs to get something to eat and the TV was on. I saw my window burning on TV. That's right when I knew. I was shocked and my disbelief was very gone. I sat there and watched it burn and then went outside and watched them drop red dust on it and went back inside and watched some more on TV.

Then somebody asked if he could interview me for their news segment on National Public Radio. I said sure and they put about three minutes of me on the air. I had friends across the country who didn't know anything about the flood. All of a sudden my voice in Olympia, Washington, was heard by a friend while she was driving to work and she started freaking out.

Kitty: When you came back to town a couple of weeks later, did you make any effort to see if your belongings had survived?

Rex: I went down there the next day after getting back and I searched through the rubble in the daylight, somehow hoping I could find something that looked like mine. All my stuff had burned, and then after it had burned, it fell into the water and went through the flood, which probably washed through it for a week longer, so I wasn't actually expecting to find anything. I was hoping I could look at something and say; "Oh, that was my filing cabinet, that was my stove," or something. I searched for about half an hour, just walking through it, but I couldn't recognize anything at all.

Kitty: Have you since been able to replace things? I don't suppose you had something like a renter's policy?

Rex: I actually did. I was covered under my parents' insurance so I received a fair amount of money from that. FEMA and SBA have been gracious and I've had a large state grant to replace things. As far as possessions, I probably own as much as I did before the flood.

Kitty: Did you have to stand in line for the Red Cross food and things like that?

Rex: Yeah, I did. I think for the first week all I did was stand in line. I stood in line and received Red Cross vouchers for food and then started all the FEMA lines and that took forever because being a renter is a little bit different from being a home owner.

Kitty: Did you chat with any people in line?

Rex: I wasn't very communicative during that time. I was basically depressed. People from the town were surprisingly happy. I'm not a happy person in general but they were all very talkative, they were all telling stories to each other.

Kitty: People who knew each other or who didn't know each other?

Rex: Complete strangers sitting around the downtown FEMA place. You'd check in and rather than having a line they actually set up chairs, so everybody was sitting next to each other telling stories. "I lost my basement," "I lost my entire house." That was strangers who would tell each other stories. I was watching the whole thing, I didn't actually talk to anybody. Somebody new would walk in and out of the thirty people that were waiting there was always one person that knew the new person. (Laughter) Everybody knew each other somehow.

Reference:
Photograph (1997) East Grand Forks by Kennedy Bridge, by Mary Ann Draves, July 9, 1997. OGL #1351, Box 9, Folder 31. Elwyn B. Robinson Department of Special Collections, Chester Fritz Library, University of North Dakota, Grand Forks.

"Anheuser-Bush Drinking Water Can, 1997"

Reference:
Artifact (1997) Photograph by David Haeselin. OGL#1351, Box 25, Folder 3. Elwyn B. Robinson Department of Special Collections, Chester Fritz Library, University of North Dakota, Grand Forks.

911 Call

The Water is Coming

April 19th 1997, 8:26 pm
Call 566
Abstract by Samantha Criswell; quality assurance by Matthew Nelson.

Audio Link: https://perma.cc/3S58-93GP

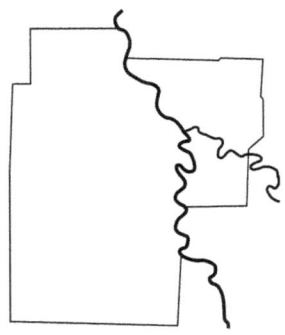

April 19th, 1997, 12:00 pm: Exactly 50 percent of Grand Forks and virtually all of East Grand Forks are flooded.

(Dialing noises, phone ringing, unintelligible voices in background)

Girl: Hello?
Dispatcher: Kelly?
Girl: Yeah.
Dispatcher: Are you home alone?
Girl: No.
Dispatcher: Are mom and dad home?
Girl: No.
Dispatcher: The water is coming.
Girl: The water's coming?
Dispatcher: It's filling up downtown area. [unintelligible noises in background] Um…all…the bank said they had it at the Lincoln Drive area…Two and a half feet…West. So be prepared if mo—are mom and dad not home?
Girl: They're coming home [unintelligible]
Dispatcher: Okay, well we have a lookout, okay? If the water rises too much give me a call?
Girl: Alright.

Dispatcher: On your street…if you have any yet?
Girl: Right on the corner of Cherry and 40th…
Dispatcher: A lot?
Girl: Well, it's enough.
Dispatcher: Okay, well just keep an eye on it and give me a call back if you need to, okay?
Girl: Alright.
Dispatcher: When mom and dad get home, give me a call if you can.
Girl: Okay.
Dispatcher: Bye.
Girl: Bye.

2

The Long Process of Recovery

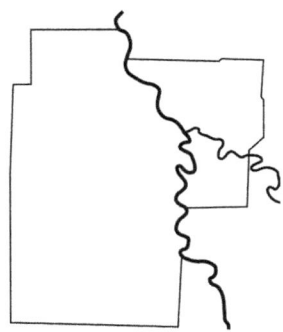

Post Flood Fight

Janet Rex

How can one convey disaster?
The spaces of loss. Nothing
flows so smoothly
as water oozing over land,
creeping through the grass,
seeping into windows, cellars,
filling streets like rivers,
basements like pools.

We peer down our cellar stairs
into a cold dark rim of wet.
Dampness breathing back at us.
We must pump this mass of liquid.
Mud and debris. Rip out these
ceiling tiles of mold,
toss our couch, chairs, books,
washer, dryer, fridge,
excavate to the shell of cement,
smells of mud and fish.

We place our belongings on the berm,
wrapped in mud and mold,

turn out these casts of our former selves
to be bulldozed away. We power wash,
scrub by hand. Tears flow,
insects erupt, and a small,
white mesh cocoon nests
upon the bedroom wall.

How can one convey disaster?
The spaces of loss. How a disaster
litters one's path with nails,
divorce, illness, death.
Toby, our brown spotted scavenger,
and Max, our golden retriever,
die, two by two, within months,
without an Ark of salvation.

How can one convey disaster?
The spaces of loss. Heart heavy.
Nerves raw. The need to fight
forward. My chest tightens
into a hard, narrow fist.

Reflections on Recovery and Tomorrow

Lynn Stauss

From *A Small Town's War: East Grand Forks' 1997 Flood Fight* (1999)

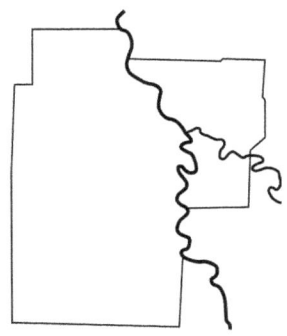

It's been two years since the Flood of the Century April 18th 1997. The buyout of homes in low-lying areas was accomplished in record setting time. This was achieved not by accident but instead was the result of an intense effort by the city of East Grand Forks.

The demolition of 450 homes moved at a rapid pace relieving family members of anxiety and stress. As the land was cleared and grass planted, new life sprang from the soil as Mother Nature reclaimed her land. For the residents only memories of neighborhoods will remain forever etched in their minds.

After the flood, East Grand Forks became a community of FEMA camping trailers and FEMA mobile homes. We became a very humble community and appreciative of the simple things in life. To this day the resilience of our residents continues to amaze me as they turned disaster and misfortune into recovery and opportunity. Many residents moved to a new location in the city, where they will begin a new life. The community has reclaimed its churches and rebuilt its schools. No where in the country will a community with a population of 8,500 have better educational opportunities. Education will be the foundation for building the future of East Grand Forks.

The residents of the city will continue to feel safer as the city provides temporary flood protection. Later the Corp of Engineers will build a permanent levee that will surround the entire community. This will provide areas of nature, wildlife, and parks with pleasing scenic views along the river.

In the next couple of years I believe East Grand Forks will experience a boom in its economic recovery in business and public facilities. For a community that has suffered financially, physically, and mentally over the past two years this will be a rewarding and emotionally uplifting experience in community pride. We will see a new business district that will provide retail shopping in East Grand Forks. Also a new government center will be built housing City Hall, County offices, and the Water and Light Department. The completion of a Park and Recreation building and a new Public Library built equipped with the most modern technology. The Firehall will also be remodeled, taking on a new look.

This summer there will be construction in every part of the city. The downtown will be completely torn upside down and inside out as the rebuilding and rebirth of our city continues.

Since the Flood a statement I have used over and over is that East Grand Forks will become "bigger and better". This dream will become reality in the next two years and all of us will be proud to claim East Grand Forks as our community.

We learned as a community that a disaster can humble us. It took away many material possessions but it didn't defeat us. We work on recovery and realize that life goes on.

The most important lesson we have learned as a community is "to do onto others as they have done onto us." Help came from all around the United States, and especially the people in Minnesota. There is no way of repaying this debt, but we can always remember them in our thoughts and prayers. We will be forever grateful to Joan (Angel) Kroc, who gave our families hope when there was nothing. We also realize how important State and Federal Government Agencies, the Red Cross, Salvation Army and the many churches, and non-profit organization are in time of disaster and recovery.

To you the residents of East Grand Forks that have asked for nothing but suffered so much, you are the survivors and the heroes from the Flood of 1997. I am proud to be your Mayor and lead you into the 21st century as we begin our new East Grand Forks.

God Bless,
    Mayor Lynn Stauss

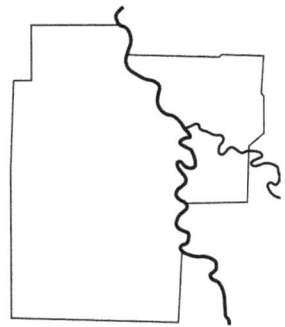

Conversation with Lynn Stauss

By the Tenth Year After, I felt like We Were Done with the Flood

David Haeselin

Lynn Stauss enjoys the view from his desk. It sits in a corner office in the West Wing of East Grand Forks, MN City Hall, erected in 2001. Like much of what the mayor can see from his window, this building was built in the years of recovery after the Flood of 1997. I talked with Mayor Stauss in that office on November 28, 2016.

East Grand Forks was hit hard by the flood, perhaps harder than anywhere else, but its downtown is now quite developed: it features new restaurants, a 15 cinema multiplex, and a Cabela's sporting goods store, what Mayor Stauss called "a destination store," clearly the feather in his recovery cap.

"Every disaster is special," he said. Stauss admitted that despite the catastrophe, the citizens of the Red River Valley, his town included, were remarkably lucky in terms of timing. "There were no wars. The economy was strong. And there were no other disasters at the time," Stauss explained.

Because they had no choice not to, Stauss tried to look at the disaster as a force to modernize and update his town. The Flood took away the "old areas," and offered opportunies for the development of new residential and recreational areas, he concluded. Stauss is particularly proud East Grand Forks' addition to the Greenway Park System, the Red River State Recreation area, a 1200-acre park which features 113 campsites, 85 of which are electric with full hookups. Nothing can bring back the five-hundred homes that were lost to develop this recreation area, but this use clearly benefits the tourists it serves and the town it represents. Stauss brags that the area is one of the few profitable recreation areas in the state of Minnesota. When I pressed him on why, he joked that it's because "we spray for mosquitoes!" He also mentioned that the area provides access to the Red River Valley, downtown Grand Forks and East Grand, and Cabela's, as well. "The first five years were terrible. By seven, I felt like we were getting things together. By the tenth year I felt we were done with the flood," he said.

When I asked about lessons we could take from the recovery, Stauss pointed to the ways that the flood brought people together. Grand Forks stood for "got flooded," East Grand Forks stood for "everybody got flooded," he quipped. Beyond that, the flood recovery brought bipartisan support. Stauss notes that both President Bill Clinton and Speaker of the House Newt Gingrich each made their way to the Red River Valley in late 1997, even while the movement to impeach Clinton was heating up. The need for recovery, it seems, was perhaps the only thing the two parties could agree upon. "Don't do it by yourself. Work together. Not as one city, one community, or one state. And after it's done, say thank you," Stauss summarized. He remains particularly proud of how young people rallied behind helping people. "It's better than protesting the election of the President," he suggested.

Stauss observed that the recovery from the flood shows how "Americans want to help each other." What's more, remembering the uncommon heroes and the heroic events of so many ordinary people that prevented a single life from being lost during the flood and the recovery of two towns and the surrounding areas can be inspiration for the power of community, state, and national collaboration. More than anything, perhaps this is the lesson we should take away from the twentieth anniversary of the Red River Flood.

On hearing my first question about what people need to know about the flood today, Stauss's eyes darted to a place on his wall. It seemed like they had made this trip many times before. He gestured to a letter written by Joan Kroc - "the Angel" - who donated $2 million to households across the valley for recovery. Fittingly, the flood chapter of the region is coming to close, if not necessarily an end. By the time you read this, Ms. Kroc will finally be officially memorialized. The road connecting the Red River State Recreation Area to downtown East Grand will be known as the Joan Kroc Memorial Roadway. Mayor Stauss retired after twenty-one years as Mayor on December 31, 2016. The view from his office stands as the legacy of what he helped rebuild.

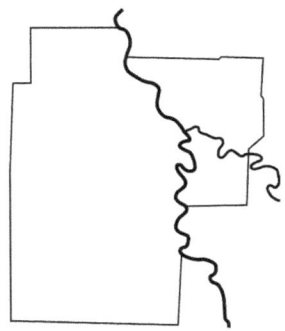

Sharks in My Basement?

Lee Murdock

The flood in the spring of 1997 was the most devastating event in the lives of many of us in the Red River Valley. It afforded us ample opportunities for tears, anxiety, and a few infrequent laughs. Two such opportunities came to us when we returned home after our evacuation.

I was a teacher by vocation and a fisherman by avocation, and thus, over the years, had amassed a fairly extensive library in both areas. That is, until the historic 1997 flood. Then all was lost in one gurgling, gushing intrusion of dirty river water into our home. Flood waters gobbled up our basement library/family room, bedroom, and bathroom.

When we returned to our home in Grand Forks after that ten day forced evacuation, I was most concerned about the amount of damage that had been done and whether or not there was anything left that was salvageable. We had begun to prepare for the cleanup while evacuating and had purchased cleaning supplies, boots, and waders. The twelve gallons of Hilex we thought we needed to kill the mold we envisioned would be infesting the walls and floor was probably overkill. There was no mold.

The waders were the first to be donned as I prepared to descend the stairs into the bowels of our home. In addition to the waders, I dressed myself in rubber gloves, a raincoat, and dust mask and carried a high intensity lantern. If anything living had made its way in with the flood waters, it certainly would have died of fright at the first glimpse of me.

As I stood at the top of the stairwell preparing to descend into the bowels of our basement, the previous surreal days fermented illogical fears in my muddled head. What types of vermin would I encounter in the murky waters below, waters that smelled a bit like soggy diapers?

I'm not sure but I think I heard the theme from Jaws playing in my head as I began my descent that day. My first surprise was how cold the water was and how dark it was at the bottom of the stairwell. When I reached the bottom of the steps, I instinctively flipped on the light switch. Of course, the electricity had been turned off by the city days ago, just before the flood waters had invaded our home. I chuckled to myself at how dumb it must have looked to be standing waist deep in river water and expecting a half-submerged light switch to do its customary job.

My lantern light illuminated the laundry room door and I sloshed toward it, sliding my feet along the carpet to be careful that I did not trip on anything that might be awaiting the opportunity to give me an unwanted dip in that putrid pool.

As I walked I was aware of objects in the water bumping against my body. I shuddered as I recalled that many huge carp and catfish inhabit the Red River. Was I being taste tested by some denizen of the deep? I consoled myself that the Red holds no known species of piranha.

I grasped the knob of the door, turned it and pushed. It sloshed slowly open. The fact that it was full of water and standing four feet deep in it, gave it an inertia that must have emulated the massive castle doors of my Scottish ancestors.

As I forced open the door, the area flooded with light from the opposite basement window and I could see that the objects that had been bumping me were books from the shelves of our library — two rooms away. At that moment I heard the voice of my wife who had been watching from the top of the stairs. "Lee," she said, "Look behind you." I turned and there floating in the murky water was one of my avocation books - I picked it up and read the title - "How To Catch Fish In Fresh Water."

We broke out laughing. It was the first time that we had shared anything except tears since wailing sirens at 2:00 A.M. on April 19th forced our evacuation. It was a welcome, much needed, momentary diversion.

Later, as we were busy cleaning out the destroyed contents of our basement, we found that our upright piano had succumbed to the water and could not be easily moved out. We decided the only way to remove it was to break it up into manageable pieces. Our son, who was helping us clean out the basement, quickly volunteered. He had haunting memories of being required to practice on it. I chuckled as I caught the gleam in his eyes and the mischievous smile on his face as he delivered each smashing blow of the sledgehammer.

During those stressful flood times, we were often given the choice of collapsing in tears or laughing at the absurdities of our situation. It was the latter that kept us sane.

"Highway Department Offices"

Reference
Donated by Joan Erickson, April - May 1997. OGL #135, Box 45, Folder 434. Elwyn B. Robinson Department of Special Collections, Chester Fritz Library, University of North Dakota, Grand Forks.

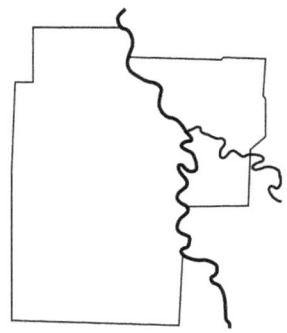

A Pint of Summer
(From the garden and freezer of Don and Shirley Naismith)

Kent Bergene

From the *North Dakota Horizons* magazine (Fall 1997)

This pint of summer comes in the form of homemade raspberry jam.

These raspberries flowered in the warm days and cool nights of summer in Grand Forks. They were watered, weeded and nurtured by Grandpa and his nine grandchildren. Upon ripening to a deep red, they were hand-picked by Grandma and the same nine grandchildren, blended into a sweet raspberry jam, and stored in the freezer. In Grandpa and Grandma's basement.

Since last summer, this pint of summer has been resting in that freezer. When the floodwater started threatening their home last week, we protected their raspberry jam with sandbags. When the water ran over the sandbags, the home became an island, surrounded by water. We protected them again with huge pumps. When the water started pouring inside, we protected them again - we taped the windows, we sandbagged the doors, and we moved the pumps inside.

Finally the water got too deep. When we were forced to leave, one of very few things we carried out was this pint of summer. We placed it in a Styrofoam cooler with a few of its friends. We set the Styrofoam cooler in Grandma and Grandpa's canoe, and we paddled away.

The floodwater chased us away, but it didn't beat us. Just as every person in Grand Forks escaped the floodwater safely, so every jar of Grandma and Grandpa's jam is safe too.

If this disastrous flood has left a bitter taste in your mouth, this pint of summer can help you remember all that is sweet in this part of the world. If you want a taste of home, this pint of summer can bring it to you. If you want to help, this is a way to pitch in.

May God bless you all.

(This poem was read during Minneapolis' WCCO radio's flood auction in April. The pint of jam sold for $175.)

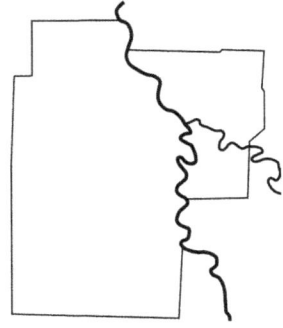

A Conversation with Ken Vein

I'm Glad that you Don't Associate Grand Forks with the Flood!

Michala Prigge

In defining Grand Forks' future, Ken Vein refuses to settle on one single idea. Perhaps his reticence is a byproduct of having spent the twenty years since the flood dealing with many complex problems requiring decisions that were guaranteed to anger someone. Building a flood protection system, wall, and floodplain capable of withstanding 500-year flood water levels, for instance, meant condemning the homes still standing in the proposed plain. Grand Forks' recovery required countless decisions about the relationship of wants of individuals versus the needs of the many.

Mr. Vein and I had met before the conversation that I describe below. We met a city council meeting where he, and others, were defending their decision to build a new downtown apartment complex in Arbor Park, a small pocket park made after the original structure had been removed after the flood. Today, Arbor Park features a stature commemorating the flood. Just as in the immediate aftermath from the flood, city leaders are focusing on downtown. Vein and the city council's plans prioritize smarter development of the downtown area to encourage, in their words, density and diversity. These plans hope to carry on the successful development the Greenway flood protection and park system that now stands one of the region's top attractions.

During our conversation, Vein repeatedly stressed that it took the concerted effort of many different people to get Grand Forks back to where it is today. He explained that the city's recovery was not without its hardships; times were trying for every member of the community during the spring of 1997 and the following years. Vein himself was viewed by some as a hero when it came to his involvement in the flood, and he was also compared to Hitler by others. The wide range of perspectives on those in power is to be expected during any natural disaster, especially one as devastating as the flood of 1997.

As the city's lead engineer, it was Vein's job to develop and enforce new codes before owners in the downtown area could rebuild and reopen. This process included filling in most basements so that this type of damage did not happen again. Foresight and planning is essential for long-term recovery, but that is often hard to appreciate from the perspective of someone whose business is sitting unused or whose home is sitting vacant awaiting demolition.

Change is a difficult thing for anyone, especially for traditionalist North Dakotans, who wanted nothing more than to return to normalcy after losing their homes, their belongings and their sense of identity. In the face of all of this pain, Vein reminded me that many positives came through recovery; with the Greenway and the pocket parks scattered around the downtown area, the city created vibrant spaces out of those that could have easily been forgotten. According to Vein, there were even talks of moving the historic downtown area of Grand Forks. Instead, he and the city council, chose to fight for it. And Vein continues to fight for his vision for downtown today.

Vein's most memorable moments of the flood all relate to processing the sheer amount of damage. Standing on the levees, he watched the water coming through, making the place he calls home become indistinguishable from the river. He will never forget the families sandbagging dikes around their homes in hopes they would be intact when they returned. Many lives hung in the balance, and Vein remains extremely proud today that no lives were lost.

The first task of the recovery process for Vein and the city engineers was compiling worst case scenarios. After taking stock in this way, it became clear that there were many steps required for successfully rebuilding and protecting the city. Vein and the engineers decided to start with getting infrastructure up to code before families could start gutting their homes and salvaging their belongings. Throughout the rebuilding process there were many issues with code violations and redistribution of land. Many decisions were made for the city of Grand Forks and not for individual families, therefore some were left feeling forgotten and distrustful of those in power. These decisions about "wants versus needs" were up to Vein and other city council members to make, creating a complex emotional and political environment for those eager to rebuild and settle back into their homes. After making sure the town was livable again, Vein understood his team's responsibility as creating a sustainable flood protection plan along with the Army Corps of Engineers. Their collaborative efforts led to the creation of a 212 year flood plan around the Greater Grand Forks Greenway, offering both recreation spaces and features that further reinforce protection. Vein also explained that new levees are prepared for ice, and have almost an extra seven feet of protection.

All told, Grand Forks' current flood protection should withstand water levels up to the 500-year flood levels. For comparison, Fargo, ND (just 70 miles downriver of Grand Forks) is currently only protected up to the 100-year level. Fargo also experienced record flooding levels during 1997, but remained safe from truly catastrophic water levels because of various meteorological and hydrological factors. If Fargo today were hit with the same proportional levels as Grand Forks did during the 1997, the metropolitan area (including Moorhead, Minnesota on the other side of the Red) of over 200,000 people would be at great risk. It must be noted that the infrastructural investment secured during the recovery effort allowed Vein and his team to build a state of the art flood protection system. Nature will continue to be unpredictable, but the citizens of Grand Forks are far better protected than they were in the spring of 1997.

Just as the people of Grand Forks have needed to adjust and evolve in the wake of the disaster, Vein shared with me that he has consulted with representatives from other recovery efforts from Hurricane Katrina in New Orleans and Iowa flooding of 2008. The successful planning and rebuilding of Grand Forks has been recognized by other regions and states throughout the past twenty years. Looking back to the pronounced distrust, paranoia, and anger of residents immediately after the flood, this sense of security and trust in the flood protection and city government is truly remarkable. On this note, Vein concluded that Grand Forks should be thought of a model for other cities experiencing devastation and rightly so. However, it is essential for us to also keep in mind the unique circumstances that Grand Forks and the Red River Valley faced. As other contributors in this collection have noted, the timing of the flood worked to the advantage in the Valley's recovery. The amount of recovery money delivered to the city exceeded expectations because there were few other disasters or wars during that time.

During our conversation, Vein was always quick to remember the work his peers and neighbors. He is still proud to be part of type of community that made it through such upheaval, and was happy to do his part to help guide others through the journey he will never forget. And with this work consulting with other flood-affected places, citizens can be sure that the lessons learned by Grand Forks are helping others flood develop strategies for the most widespread and efficiency recoveries possible.

Vein believes Grand Forks is steadily growing into who they once were; its future is up to its people. When I asked him about the uses of memory, he replied that it is important to remember the flood, but it is even more important to move on and begin advancing the infrastructure of Grand Forks. This is reason why he advocates building an apartment complex where Arbor Park now resides. To his mind, downtown was successfully saved and the sacrifice that it required should inspire continued prosperity and growth.

The flood happened, and Arbor park is a product of that, but, according to Vein, "that was then and this is now." Vein contends that the city, especially downtown, must focus on growth, density, and infrastructure, using the successful growth of the south end of town as inspiration. While this argument may fail to convince the group of citizens that have emerged to save the park, or the Grand Forks Historic Preservation committee, for that matter, Vein's continued passion for Grand Forks is unmistakable. Vein has dedicated much of his adult life towards ensuring a better future for Grand Forks and its community and anyone who cares about Grand Forks today can still learn much from his example.

"FEMA Show Me The Money!!!"

Reference:
Photographed by David Haeselin. OGL #1351, Box 24, Folder 3. Elwyn B. Robinson Department of Special Collections, Chester Fritz Library, University of North Dakota, Grand Forks.

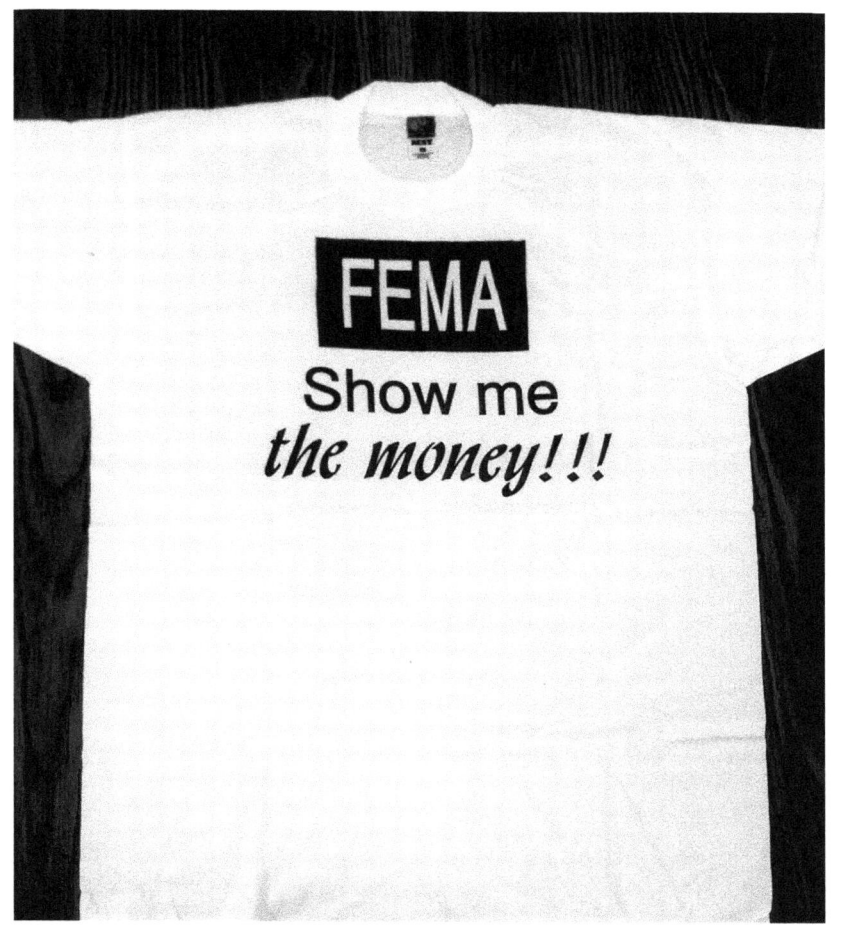

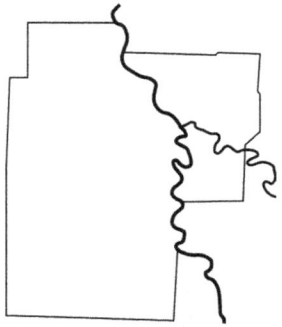

911 Call

FEMA

April 18th, 1997, 8:36 pm
Call 658
Abstract by Samantha Criswell
Quality assurance by Matthew Nelson.

Audio Link: https://perma.cc/EZ4B-64E9

April 18th 1997, 8:08 p.m.: National Weather Service revises crest for 54.0 feet.

Dispatcher: Law enforcement center.
Caller: Hi, say, I'm trying to find out some information for some people down in Riverside Park area?
Dispatcher: That should be all evacuated.
Caller: It is.
Dispatcher: Yep, Riverside area is totally evacuated.
Caller: They're putting up a dike, and…are they planning on putting any clean water in the basements?
Dispatcher: I have no idea. I think the residents have to recover the basements. They're probably full, I would assume by now. There's water coming through in a lot of areas. But, those areas have been mandatory evacuated this morning.
(phones ringing in background)
Caller: I know. I live down there too.
Dispatcher: Okay.
Caller: Do you know…is there anybody from FEMA that I can contact on this…on this water stuff?
Dispatcher: Yep, if you look on channel three there's a 1-800 number that comes across with the FEMA number—

Caller: I'm at a business office.

Dispatcher: Okay, I don't have the number right in here. Uh…

Caller: Okay, I've had…I sell insurance and I live down there and the people are turning to me for information, and the 800 numbers I have are Monday through Friday numbers.

Dispatcher: Um, I think that might be the same. Between 8 and 6?

Caller: Probably.

Dispatcher: I think that's what I have. The last rumors are, what I have heard, was if a law enforcement official or if an official tells you that you would be better ahead to put water in your basement…then, um, that they could do that. That's what I had heard.

Caller: But then that's – that's what would cover it?

Dispatcher: That's what I had been told, um, I can give you the number to EOC and they might be able to have a better number for you.

Caller: I can't get through there, I've been trying and trying and trying.

Dispatcher: [1:19?] But that's the best that we can do. I'm sorry I don't have many more information.

Caller (deep sigh): Uhhhhh…okay.

Dispatcher: Okay?

Caller: Thank you.

Dispatcher: Yep.

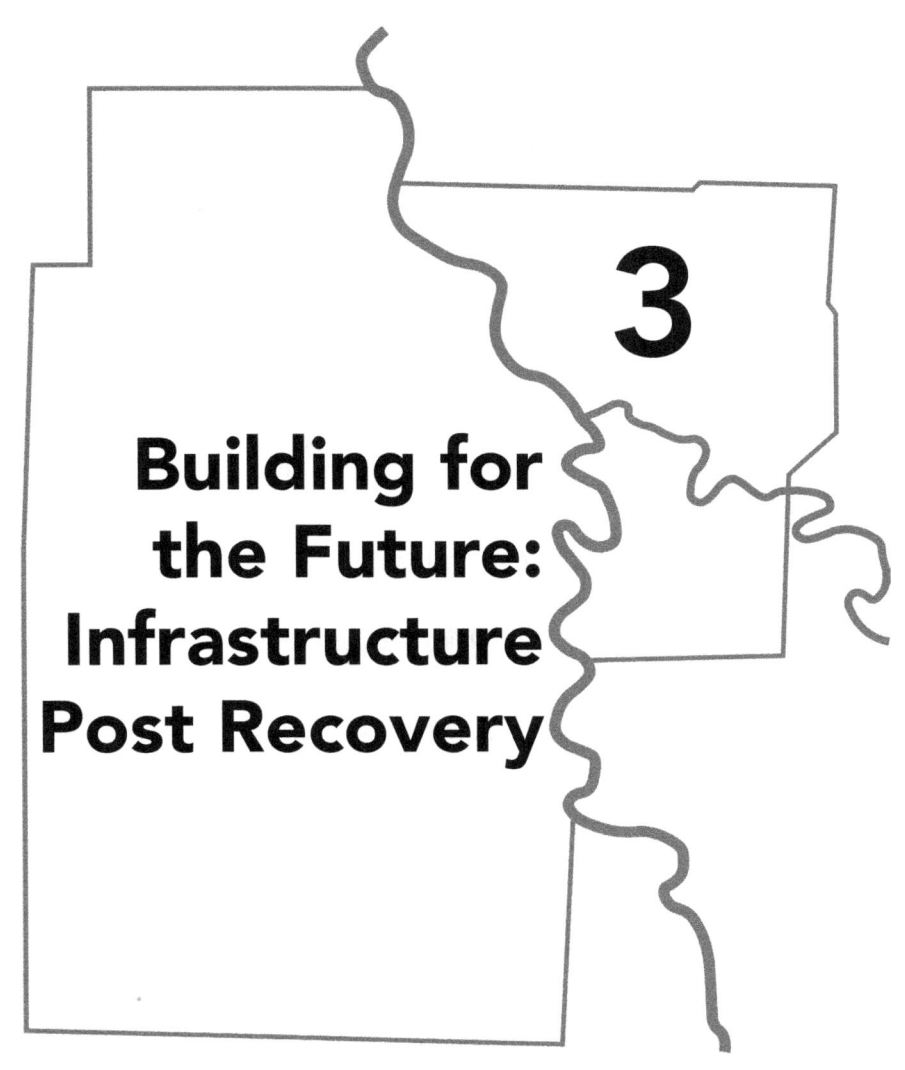

3

Building for the Future: Infrastructure Post Recovery

"Final Draft of Proposed Structure of the Greenway"

Reference:
Greenway Renaissance. OGL #1351, Box 3, Folder 63. Elwyn B. Robinson Department of Special Collections, Chester Fritz Library, University of North Dakota, Grand Forks.

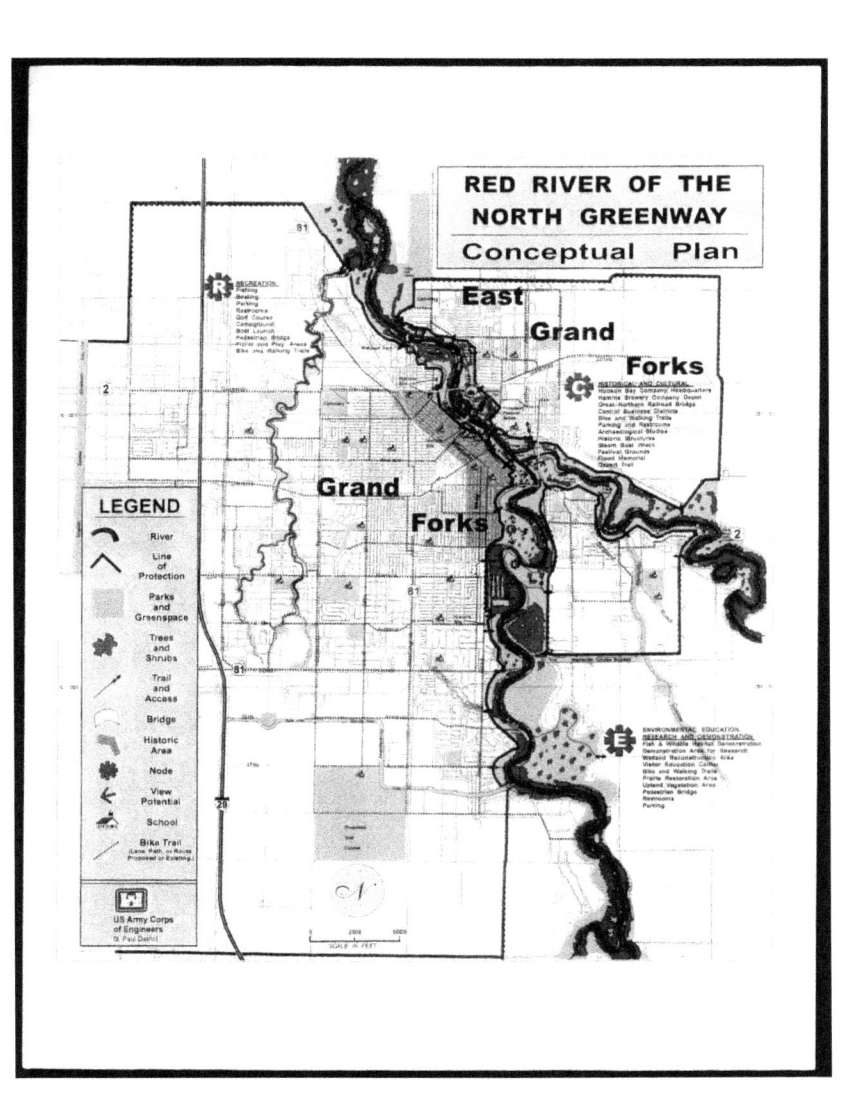

THE RED RIVER GREENWAY
US ARMY CORPS OF ENGINEERS

INTRODUCTION

The initial concept of the Red River Greenway was part of a flood control proposal prepared by the US Army Corps of Engineers, Saint Paul District (Corps). The proposal, prepared in response to requests from the North Dakota Congressional delegation, was to mitigate impacts to the Greater Grand Forks area from flooding along the Red River of the North and the Red Lake River. The proposal defines a strategy for protecting the cities from future floods and provides a recreational amenity for residents of the Greater Grand Forks area.

OVERVIEW

The flood protection plan presented by the Corps will protect the cities from floods of a magnitude equal to the 1997 flood. This will be accomplished by the erection of a system of levees. The levees will extend along the banks of both rivers and either tie into high ground or completely encircle the cities. Because of unstable soils along the riverbanks, the levees must be built away from the rivers, on stable ground.

The Greenway Concept Plan calls for a greenway to be located on the floodplains of the Red River and Red Lake River between the cities of Grand Forks, North Dakota and East Grand Forks, Minnesota. The greenway is accommodated between the proposed levee systems and encompasses about 2,000 acres of floodway. The plan in its simplest form proposes construction of a series of 'green' spaces connected by a trail system. In its most complex form it could include lighted plazas connecting to the cities and park like areas for gatherings and recreation. The concept provides the residents of the cities a unique opportunity to help shape the redevelopment of their cities by incorporating a green (natural) element into those areas most ravaged by the recent flooding.

Reference:
U.S. Army Corps of Engineers. undated, ca.1998-1999. OGL #1351, Box 3, Folder 58. Elwyn B. Robinson Department of Special Collections, Chester Fritz Library, University of North Dakota, Grand Forks.

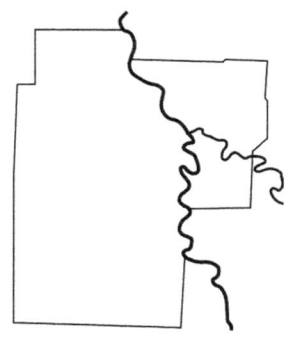

Document:

The Red River Greenway

U.S. Army Corps of Engineers

INTRODUCTION

The initial concept of the Red River Greenway was part of a flood control proposal prepared by the US Army Corps of Engineers, Saint Paul District (Corps). The proposal, prepared in response to requests from the North Dakota Congressional delegation, was to mitigate impacts to the Greater Grand Forks area from flooding along the Red River of the North and the Red Lake River. The proposal defines a strategy for protecting the cities from future floods and provides a recreational amenity for residents of the Greater Grand Forks area.

OVERVIEW

The flood protection plan presented by the Corps will protect the cities from floods of a magnitude equal to the 1997 flood. This will be accomplished by the erection of a system of levees. The levees will extend along the banks of both rivers and either tie into high ground or completely encircle the cities. Because of unstable soils along the riverbanks, the levees must be built away from the rivers, on stable ground.

The Greenway Concept Plan calls for a green way to be located on the floodplains of the Red River and Red Lake River between the cities of Grand Forks, North Dakota and East Grand Forks, Minnesota. The greenway is accommodated between the proposed levee systems and encompasses about 2,000 acres of floodway. The plan in its simplest form proposes construction of a series of 'green' spaces connected by a trail system. In its most complex form it could include lighted plazas connecting to the cities and park like areas for gatherings and recreation.

The concept provides the residents of the cities a unique opportunity to help shape the redevelopment of their cities by incorporating a green (natural) element into those areas most ravaged by the recent flooding.

GREENWAY CONCEPT

This plan is a concept; its purpose is to elicit comment and discussion on the floodway proposal. The thesis of the plan is that the area between the cities' levees and/or flood walls could be available for some forms of recreation or other uses. It presents a single possibility of what could be; there are many possibilities. Keeping in mind that the area must first function as a floodway, this concept leans heavily towards an environmentally friendly, low maintenance approach with trails, few structures or high maintenance areas, a lot of floodplain restoration and many natural open areas.

The basis of the design idea is that the greenway will have three primary areas of influence: Cultural, Recreation, and Environmental. As a way of organizing these components into workable design alternatives, we have centered them in three areas of the greenway. These three elements are presented as nodes in the plan. The "Nodes" are simply the focus of areas of influence. They fit naturally into the present structure of the cities and overlap to some extent. The Nodes are interconnected by an extensive trail system that runs the length of the project on both sides of the river(s) and is linked by three pedestrian bridges spanning the Red River. The trail concept provides for city to city connection and multiple neighborhood accesses.

The Recreation Node is centered at the downstream end of the project where some existing recreation features could be incorporated and connected. Recreation trails would provide access to the entire project but most active recreation features will be moved behind the line of protection. Recreation trails could connect existing community recreation features.

Recreation often is thought of in terms of sports (such as baseball, football, tennis, etc.). In reality, only a very small portion of the population participates in these types of activities. Of much more use to the population in general are areas where the more passive recreation activities are appropriate. The recreation aspects of the concept embrace those types of recreation that are compatible with the project. In addition to the trail system and community open spaces, other areas that support informal recreation could be designed throughout the Greenway as a series of connected spaces. These spaces will allow for informal physical activity but, of much greater importance - they will also work as a floodway - allowing floodwater to flow with little restriction.

The Historical and Cultural Node is centered between the business districts of the cities. Its purpose is to provide spaces for cultural and historical celebration and a dedicated area to present the historical and cultural aspects of both cities.

The greenway could also be used as an education resource for the local schools and the university. The concept offers an active opportunity for outdoor classrooms connected to the greenway by a city trail system. It could be an excellent resource for supplementing the education curriculums for natural sciences, engineering, and landscape ecology.

The Environmental Node includes the upstream areas of the project. It shows a buffer strip on the east bank of the river, south of the East Grand Forks levees. The main idea here is to present the river in as natural a state as possible. This would preclude most types of development and would require restoration of the natural riverine ecosystem.

As the Red River is on one of the primary north-to-south flyways for migratory birds on the North American continent, it is expected that, with the re-establishment of natural habitat, native bird and animal populations would become important contributors to the ambiance of the greenway. Again, this would provide the local schools with the opportunity to provide "hands-on" learning experiences for the students.

The "Fingers of Green" is an important part of the concept. It refers to that part of the design that will tie the green way directly into the neighborhoods and the downtown areas of the cities. The proposed trail system will provide connections to the coulees that intersect the cities (English, Hartsville, and Belmont) and will also link directly to the hearts of both cities with street and pedestrian accesses. Part of the idea is to connect with streets that have special landscape amenities installed such as distinctive lighting, extra parking, pedestrian benches, and special landscape plantings (i.e., "green streets").

RED RIVER GREENWAY VISION STATEMENT

The Red River Greenway will protect the residents of Grand Forks and East Grand Forks from flooding, provide opportunities for economic growth, improve and restore ecological stability to the river corridor, link residents and tourists to four-seasons of recreation and transportation facilities, provide linkage between the cities, preserve and promote the history and culture of the region through education, and improve the quality of life for future generations.

Red River Greenway Workshop, February, 1998

THE GREENWAY PLANNING PROCESS

After the flood protection proposal was presented to Congress, additional planning measures for the proposal and the Greenway Concept were implemented. In January, 1998, an initial planning workshop for the Greenway was held in Grand Forks. At this meeting, the Greenway Concept, the Corps planning process, and our vision (examining the potential of the concept) were presented to local, state, and national representatives of the government and concerned groups. During this meeting, the invitees were asked to list their opinions, concerns, and desires. The second planning workshop, in February, was facilitated by Mr. Charles (Chuck) Flink, President of Greenways Incorporated, an internationally recognized expert on greenway planning, design, implementation, and management. During the February meeting, the Goals and Objectives were refined, key issues, appropriate facilities, and an action plan were discussed. The group also defined a Vision Statement for the Red River Greenway. This current workshop, March 11-12, 1998, is also facilitated by Mr. Flink. Its purposes are to get your opinion (what would you like to see happen in these areas of the floodway?) and also further refine the information we have gathered to this date (what do you think of the Vision Statement, did we miss an important Goal or Objective?, etc.).

GREENWAY GOALS AND OBJECTIVES

From this vision statement, specific goals and objectives were defined that will be used to implement the greenway. Goals define key strategies of the vision. Objectives define how the goals might best be achieved.

Goal 1 - Promote and Develop Greenway

Objectives:
- Build support for this concept keeping in mind the safety and flood protection properties of the original concept must be the first consideration of any plan.
- Develop common link or bond and sense of belonging or ownership to help unify the communities.
- Integrate local, County, State and Federal plans for communities adjacent to the Red River and Red Lake River.
- Develop governing structure that allows for a wide variety of compatible uses.
- Insure that approved amenities will be flood proof and compatible with the floodplain.

- Develop a multi-use greenway flexible to change.
- Ensure that The Red River Greenway is included as part of the Community Conversation dialogue.
- Get the community involved in the master planning and design for the greenway.

Goal 2 - Support and Enhance the Community

Objectives:
- Support economic development.
- Create a festive atmosphere for year round activities.
- Create space and activities that bring community together.
- Focus on the arts and create spaces for the display of art.
- Make sure the greenway is open to downtown amenities.
- Promote tourism throughout the four-seasons with attractions and activities.
- Provide aesthetic transitions from levees to neighborhoods.
- Create beautiful areas that serve the public.
- Preserve and protect aesthetic resources.
- Keep the greenway appropriately maintained and managed.
- Make greenway development consistent and supportive of East Grand Forks and Grand Forks downtown redevelopment plans.

Goal 3 - Promote Partnering

Objectives:
- Build federal, state, county, and local partnerships to support the greenway.
- Determine management partners before design and development.
- Consider regulatory and permit requirements.
- Select partnering groups for governing.
- Build partnerships with community groups, organizations, neighborhoods, schools, etc.
- Define an 'evangelist' who will champion the Greenway Plan and see it through to completion.
- Coordinate community redevelopment with plans for the greenway.

- Assemble a steering committee to guide overall development process (River Forks Commission could be a lead partner).
- Define a structure that allows for and promotes individualism within the overall structure of greenway implementation.

Goal 4 - Enhance, Protect, and Restore the Environment

Objectives:
- Activities along the river corridors should minimize adverse effects on water quality, fish and wildlife, vegetation, bank stability, stream flow, visual qualities, noise, and safety.
- Promote public awareness of the river.
- Emphasize the value of riparian corridor.
- Improve ecological stability of the river corridor.
- Use native species where prudent
- Provide a wildlife corridor that links habitat patches.
- Restore fish migration and spawning habitat.
- Improve water quality & aquatic life.
- Provide non-point source water treatment.
- Manage drainage to enhance the riverine ecosystem.
- Provide four-season outdoor learning experiences for all age groups.
- Promote low maintenance for natural areas.
- Use 'soft engineering' design solutions.

Goal 5 - Preserve and Promote Cultural and Historical Heritage

Objectives:
- Provide historic interpretation and education through wayside exhibits.
- Preserve cities' and region's history.
- Preserve, through relocation, historic structures.
- Interpret, through 'Type C' visitor center, flood history and local and regional history.
- Soften impact of 20 foot high floodwalls.

Goal 6 - Maximize Recreation Opportunities and Promote a Healthy Lifestyle

Objectives:
- Provide a variety of recreational facilities, including river-oriented opportunities.
- Provide for four-season use (winter activities).
- Mitigate existing recreation in the floodplain and relocate.
- Provide as many diverse recreation opportunities as possible.
- Provide large open spaces for public use.
- Provide roads and parking facilities.
- Future paths for hiking, biking, etc.
- Provide low maintenance facilities.
- Provide sites for peace, mental welfare and well-being.
- Be sensitive to the upheaval, trauma, and disruption of lives from the '97 flood.
- Provide universally accessible trail system.
- Provide trail accesses adjacent to retirement centers.
- Encourage private development near the greenway.
- Provide access to the greenway and between neighborhoods through the flood control structures.
- Connect the cities with additional river crossings.
- Use "Fingers of Green" concept to connect area businesses and residences in both communities.
- Link greenway uses.

MARCH FORUMS

Agenda:

Wednesday, March 11th in the Lecture Bowl on the 2nd floor:
12:00 - 5:00 PM Public Open House - displays of Greenway Concept Plan, Vision Statement, Goals and Objectives, and greenway images.
6:00 - 7:00 PM Presentation, "Benefits of Greenways" by Charles A. Flink, President of Greenways Inc.
7:00 - 8:00 PM Questions and answers - wrap-up

Thursday, March 12th in the Alumni Room on the 2nd floor:
8:00 AM - 2:00 PM Public Open House.
2:00 - 4:00 PM Focus Group meeting.
4:00 PM Wrap-up, adjourn.

The previous meetings on the Red River Greenway were aimed at finding a focus for the Greenway Concept. The direction chosen, to this point in the planning process, has been towards a greenway that must first function as a floodway, designed with few structures or high maintenance areas, with a multi-purpose trail system, is environmentally friendly, restores floodplain habitat, and has many natural open areas.

This meeting is being held to gather the thoughts and feelings of the community- this means you. We want to know what your priorities are - your values - your vision of Greater Grand Forks in the years ahead. This meeting is being held specifically so that you can be heard. We welcome your thoughts, ideas, concerns, and comments on the Red River Greenway Concept.

PROJECT COSTS

The US Army Corps of Engineers reports to the Congress of the United States; it is the that Congress allocates funding and also legislates how the Corps distributes the costs of flood control projects it is involved with. Congress has mandated that the costs of flood control projects be shared between the Federal Government and the recipient of the project (sponsor). For the Greater Grand Forks Flood Control Project, cost sharing responsibilities have been established as a 50/50 split between the government/sponsor for the flood protection aspects of the project. A 50/50 cost sharing is also required for the recreation components of the plan. As there are other factors involved in the computations, recreation is recorded as a separate cost. The Corps is also limited in what recreation amenities it can cost-share with the sponsor. The poster titled Checklist of Recreation Facilities the Corps of Engineers Can Provide lists the recreation features that can be cost-shared if all other requirements are met. Features other than those listed can be built but the sponsor is responsible for 100% of the cost of any feature that is not listed or does not meet all of the requirements.

We thank you for your input and support. Please contact us if you have comments or questions.

"Levee Alignments:
Northridge Hills Court Option of a Floodwall"

Reference:
Grand Forks Public Works. OGL #1351, Box 17, Folder 15.
Elwyn B. Robinson Department of Special Collections, Chester Fritz Library, University of North Dakota, Grand Forks.

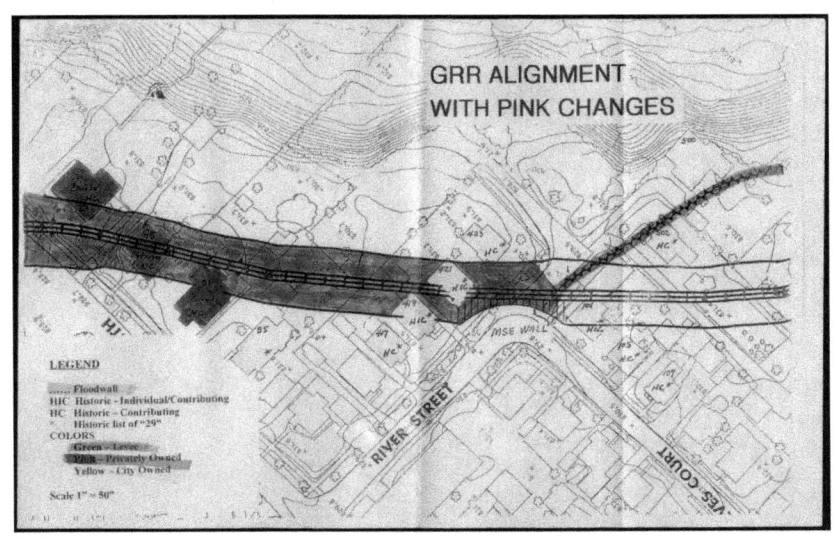

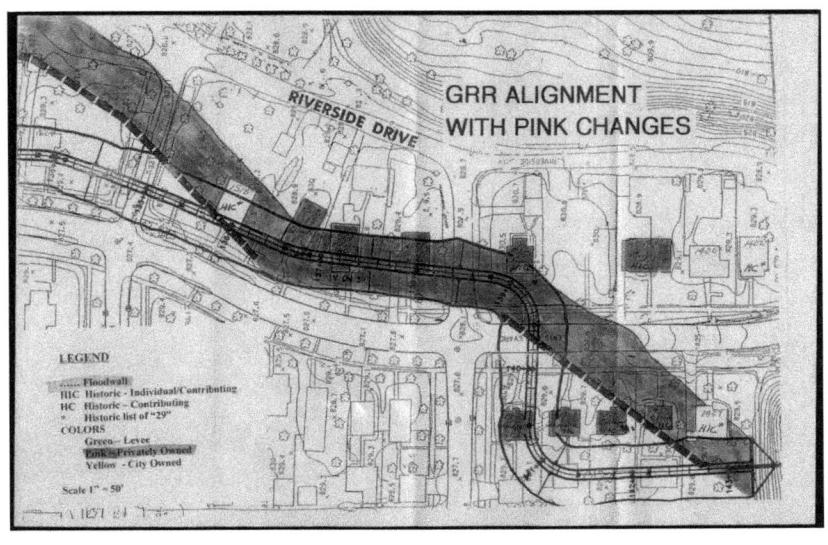

Habitat Home

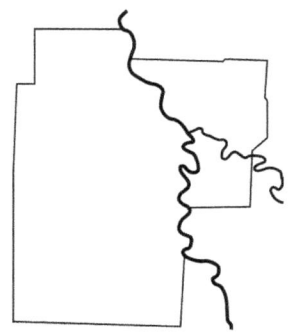

Janet Rex

I reach into water, thick as silk,
placing this beat of a blue pump
into an excavation of clay, reddish,
newly scratched by a large yellow cat,
and dug up by a shovel claw. Rainwater,
filling the hole, reflects stray clouds

like faces hovering. Siphoned water
gushes through the garden hose.
Soon a house pushes up
through concentric, footing rings, rising
through block wall like a beehive,
as a flurry of workers scurry in and out

over chutes and ladders. I feed them grapes
with the daily fare, and they cite
Christian, Mormon, and other creeds
as they lay drain tile
like a black guardian snake
in pea rock near the footings.

They tar block walls with Neolithic color.
Some plumb, lay floors,
and from the surrounds of sawdust
at the peaks of the cathedral ceiling,
blond beams arise
like spider webs under those long-legged

volunteers, laying their pattern
of wood, siding, shingles, insulation,
poly. They wrap the walls tight as flies.
They sheetrock, tape, texture, paint,
as I caress sandpaper across doors and trim
until they're smooth as skin. I scatter a dust

of fine shavings, before five Hutterites
ease fruitwood stain on walnut trim,
then lunch perched along the scaffolding,
flag-like scarves fluttering. On that Labor Day,
insulation flies out beneath the eaves
to catch upon the scaffolding

like white, heralding moths, or a wild
shower of bees, while I polyurethane
a thick honey on doors and trim. The swarm
of workers returns—electricians,
plumbers, a host of heating experts,
carpet layers. In the postequinox cold,

electricians, who swirl in like lightning
stringing their multicolored wiring,
must finish in the fuse-blown dark
like fireflies with their flashlights. They
draw out a slender thread
from a skein of rainbow energy,

and in a breath, the house
alights. This grayling,
cradled in clay above the water table,
is blessed by our softest murmuring,
and a priest's sprinkling of holy water,
before it's passed to the chosen family

like a dream fluttering through the crowd.
My hands fold and open, fold and open,
clapping, for this newborn home lying
in the midst of ribbons of concrete,
filled with cabinets like cocoons,
and carpeted the color of moth wings.

"402 Chestnut"

Reference:
Alan Draves. Photograph. OGL #1351, Box 17, Folder 58, Item 1523. Elwyn B. Robinson Department of Special Collections, Chester Fritz Library, University of North Dakota, Grand Forks.

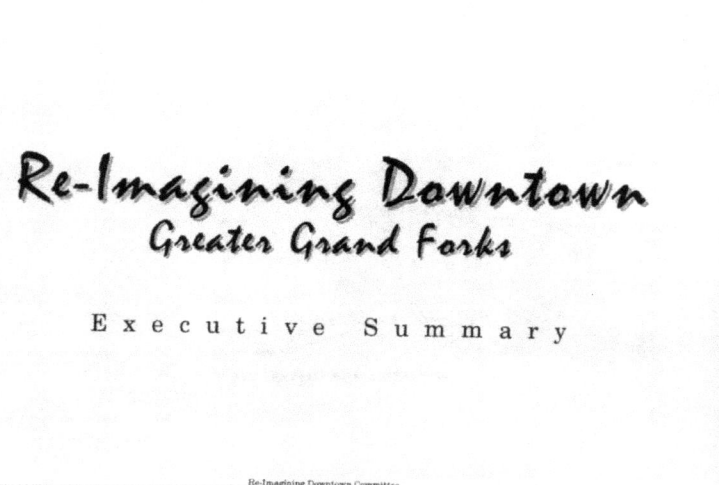

Reference:
Atelier Heamavihio. 1997. OGL #1351, Box 3, Folder 58. Elwyn B. Robinson Department of Special Collections, Chester Fritz Library, University of North Dakota, Grand Forks.

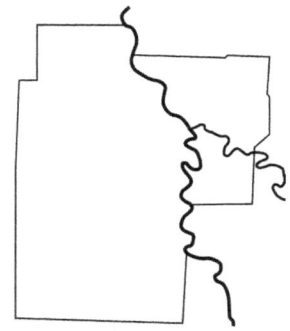

Document:

Re-Imagining Downtown Greater Grand Forks

U.S. Army Corps of Engineers

INTRODUCTION

A very exciting and wonderful thing happened on the way to today. The citizen's of Greater Grand Forks created a collective vision for the rebirth of their downtowns, a reimagining, if you will.

On May 13, 1997 The Mayor's Task Force on Business Redevelopment was formed to spearhead efforts at re-establishing Greater Grand Forks. One sub-committee, ReImagining Downtown, was created specifically to address the special needs of the downtowns of East Grand Forks and Grand Forks. Through their efforts and the efforts of the citizens of Greater Grand Forks a new vision of the downtown was created. This vision is grounded in both optimism and Mid-West conservatism as it should be. It proposes a remarkable view of a vibrant, united city that embraces its joining river. This collective vision is seen as the framework, the organizer, for continued planning throughout the region. It will undoubtedly change. But that is the nature of a good master plan. The basic ideas are sound. The vision is remarkably clear.

This document presents an executive summary of the work that has been accomplished. The ideas, creativity, and vision presented here are the result of the Re-Imagining Downtown Charrette which took place on June 28, 29 & 30 in City Council Chambers

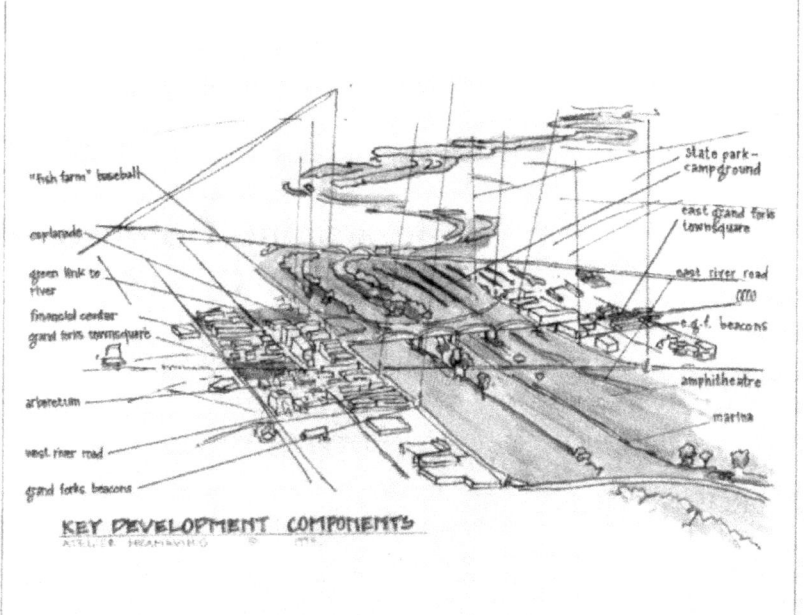

KEY DEVELOPMENT COMPONENTS

in Grand Forks. This charrette engaged the public from Grand Forks and East Grand Forks in an intensive and very productive design weekend. Three overarching ideas grew out of the charrette experience and have come to galvanize the vision for downtown Greater Grand Forks.

- East Grand Forks and Grand Forks are one city. Each with unique places and needs but part of a larger whole.
- Greater Grand Forks is united by the Red River of the North.
- The downtown is a multi-use area with retail uses, office uses, entertainment, and residential uses co-existing.

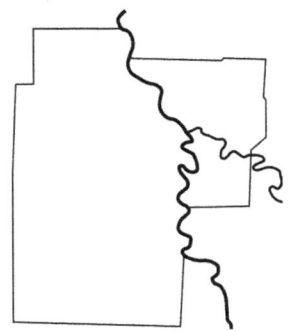

Undercurrents: Water Politics in the Red River Valley

Sherry O'Donnell

The Flood of 1997 drastically altered the cultures and economies of Grand Forks and East Grand Forks, where the Red and the Red Lake River converge before they wind north to Canada. Hundreds of working-class dwellings and the people who lived in them were washed out for good. Carpenters, electricians, hair dressers and small business owners took buyouts and moved elsewhere when federal money was steered to the south end of town. Many investors moved quickly to capitalize on the disaster, building new condos and townhouses, rezoning for hotels, industrial parks, medical centers and new shopping malls. Multi-story office buildings, dog parks, and bike trails upgraded the waterfront, now cleaned, cleared, and properly, quietly, green. The city seemed to make clear that there's no place for a noisy trailer park or an unsightly motor repair shop in the driveway. Mean dogs pacing behind chainlink fences, tricked-out pickups, three-day Cinco de Mayo parties: all gone.

Similar displacements up and down the Red River Valley, brought on by unexpected warm weather and erratic storms, have caused floods in 59 of the last 112 planting seasons in the Red River Valley. In 1997, overland flooding travelled east in Minnesota to the Lake Agassiz glacial ridge and north along the Pembina Trail. In North Dakota, water rolled north and west, following flood plains stretching over almost one-third of the state. The floods of 2003 and 2009 were particularly severe, forcing further adjustments to an increasingly unpredictable river and its tributaries. Livestock and crop losses drove smaller farms and towns out of business. Land acquisition by large growers and investors reduced rural populations and suburbanized large swaths of land. New homeowners turned pastures and ditches into vast, well-tended lawns. School bus routes grew longer and post offices closed as rural populations shrank. Multi-hyphenated signs on the busses marked efforts to consolidate schools and keep sports teams viable; grandparents decided to winter in Florida or Arizona or Mexico while civic, church, and community volunteers grew scarce.

All of these changes were well underway fifty years ago, but post-1997 realignments of cultures and economies have turned land into real estate at a much faster pace, most notably in the Fargo-Moorhead area where the Flood Diversion project, begun in 2006, pushes on. Headed by the US Army Corps of Engineers and championed by urban investors who want to energize downtown, the $2.2 billion project won US congressional approval after the 2009 flood, when it offered a solution to anticipated catastrophic floods in the metro area. In the last fifteen years or so, downtown Fargo has been transformed into something resembling a Silicon Valley corporate campus: where app development and TEDx talks for young professionals thrive. In 2001, Doug Burgum sold his Great Plains software company to Microsoft, and helped make downtown Fargo a center for startup software companies, coders, and entrepreneurs. As the current governor of North Dakota, Burgum is convinced that urban professionals and inventors will revitalize the city, attracting new populations who can study, work, play and live downtown. His own company is currently encouraging similar tech campuses in downtown Grand Forks.

Scheduled for completion in 2023, The Diversion Project is hotly contested by Minnesota's Department of Natural Resources (DNR), several towns and landowners near Wahpeton, North Dakota (south of Fargo) and other upstream towns, and most urgently, by Minnesota Governor Mark Dayton. Dayton was particularly offended by the upbeat YouTube video produced by the

Fargo-Moorhead Diversion Project last August, picturing backhoes at work with no permits from Minnesota. In fact, Minnesota was not even recognized as a co-regulator of the Diversion Project. "In all my years of public service at the state and federal levels, I have never seen such a complete disregard for the process of a co-regulator," Dayton wrote in The Star Tribune.

Arguments about the safety of high-risk dams proposed by the FM Diversion project focus on environmental impacts and the design safety of various sections of the inlet structures built to take water from the diversion channel, just as Winnipeg's Red River Floodway Channel, built in the 1960's, manages overland floods headed toward the city. But the Minnesota Department of Natural Resources has refused to issue the FM Diversion a required dam permit and has also filed a lawsuit against the Corps for proceeding without it. U.S. District Judge John R. Tunheim dismissed all complaints against the Corps, but is currently reconsidering arguments by the Richland-Wilkin group, the Minnesota DNR, and Governor Dayton, who has made watershed projects for rivers and lakes a major environmental priority all over the state.

Conflicts between the US Army Corps of Engineers and local farmers, environmentalists, native tribal councils, and rural towns are frequent and longstanding. A particularly instructive example occurred after the flood of 1969, when the Corps proposed the construction of a spillway dam on the Red Lake River in Louisville Township, Minnesota. The proposed emergency spillway would allow overland flooding of farms and towns all along the Red Lake River, from Crookston to Red Lake Falls. For seven years, the Corps pushed its dam diversion project. It was finally abandoned only after local farmers and city officials conclusively proved that the spillway design literally rested on quicksand and unstable aquifers.

Given the political and environmental impact of proposed future projects, one must ask how Louisville Township (population 1,359) managed to block this proposed spillway dam. More specifically, one needs to ask how was this project, presented as the only modern and sensible guarantee against looming catastrophic floods, stopped by local citizens who knew the Corps claims were inaccurate? Futhermore, how did these citizens, who shared some but not all of each others' concerns, manage to organize and win control of public policy affecting their land and their towns? In early 2017, I asked my neighbor, longtime farmer and activist, Willard Brunelle, what prompted his tireless work to oppose the Corps plan.

"It was the Larson flood of 1969," he answered. In April of that year, ice jams breeched a Red Lake River dike near Gentilly, Minnesota, six miles from the Larson farm. Water rose about three feet per minute, and neighbors, friends, and high school students helping to sandbag the Larson house and barn had to run for higher ground. A car filled with Willard's five children and their grandmother was swept into a ditch by chunks of ice. High school boys pulled the trapped children through car windows, but swift water washed some from the car rooftop. They managed to hang onto an uprooted tree until rescuers reached them about twenty minutes later. But sixty ewes and eighty new lambs had to be abandoned in the barn.

"I'll never forget the sound of those sheep drowning," Willard said. "Never."

When the Corps of Engineers plan for the Louisville Emergency spillway was proposed in 1974, Willard studied the map, saw that water would inundate the village of Gentilly, MN, travel all the way to Red Lake Falls, and cover thousands of acres of farmland in Minnesota and North Dakota. "Everyone believed that the Corps was right," Willard said. Indeed, it seems natural that people would take the government agencies' words on these manners. However, Willard continued, "I talked to the workmen, and they said that the ground they were digging was quicksand. It was nothing but quicksand. But the Corps denied this, then said the land would be condemned, so we had no choice in the matter." It seems as if political allegiances further complicated matters. "Many local mayors, those in Ada, Oslo, and Crookston as well as East Grand Forks and Grand Forks, agreed with the Corps. They said the spillway would make a wonderful tourist attraction for fishing and boating.... So I said that all the brush and trees which had to be cleared away would leave stumpage for boats to hang up on. No tourist wants to get hung up on tree stumps," Willard concluded.

Willard went to area meeting after meeting, displaying his surveying data, explaining the inaccurate measurements and poor construction designs of the Corps. Finally, one Corps engineer phoned Willard from Crookston and asked if he could drive to the Brunelle farm for a visit. He verified Willard's assessments of the Corps proposal, but warned him: "Don't say it came from me." That Corps engineer was fired six months later. "He believed in our project, said Willard. "He went back to St. Paul with our surveying map and told them and that was the end of him. The Corps drew the original map in St. Paul and never came up here."

When three farmers from Oslo managed to get elected to the city council seven years later, the Corps was finally forced to admit that quicksand, not shale, lay under the proposed dam. "We had to go through six Directors of the Corps - had a new one every year - until we got an agreement, said Willard. One Oslo City Council member got so mad that the proposed damn lost that she "took her cane and whipped it on the table. 'If it would not be for some other people around here we'd have our dam'."

This history of dealing with the politics of water encouraged Willard to bring his expertise to fighting floods. "I got involved in the 1997 Flood because I knew we didn't have a plan. I went to a planning meeting in Crookston and learned they were worried about how much time we would have for evacuation. They said two hours. I knew that was wrong," Willard told me. Again, Willard attended meeting after meeting, listened to what city, county, and regional officials had to say. He listened carefully, and then suggested that a plane be used to survey flood waters and provide a more accurate estimate of the rising rates, flow patterns of flooding rivers and tributaries. Most importantly, ice jams could be located more quickly. He suggested that the Civil Air Patrol in Thief River Falls be enlisted, then volunteered to accompany the pilot on each trip, filming the river and overland floods.

Beginning on April 9, 1997, Willard flew five times over Polk, Red Lake, Marshall, and Norman counties with the Civil Air Patrol, taking photos and measurements for county officials. He was soon joined by a newly-arrived FEMA representative, who sent her copies of Willard's reports to FEMA Headquarters in Washington, D.C.

"My radio handle was Air Mobile One," Willard chuckled. "When Air Force One carrying President Clinton flew into Grand Forks Air Base I radioed for clearance."

On the ground, Willard was busy organizing shelter for flood evacuees. 1,400 stayed in churches, schools, and family homes in Crookston and the surrounding area. His Marine Corps buddies stuffed stock trailers with toys, warm clothing, and more toys to distribute to shelters. Volunteers sat at a long phone table in the police station, taking calls for help of all kinds.

"The most important part, and the dirtiest and most depressing part of flood work, is the cleanup," said Willard. "In 1969, we cleaned up the Larson farm for three weeks. All those dead sheep. All that wet grain. All that stuff." Many taut the fact that no person lost their lives during the flood, but that doesn't mean that there were no casualties.

Willard's experiences show firsthand how bureaucracy works within and sometimes against infrastructural improvements. "After the dam project was defeated, we wanted a new bridge down at Huot. We had lost the old one with the ice jams so the Feds were supposed to pay half. The Red Lake County engineer was getting nowhere, so he told us to write letters to the feds. We did. We explained that we need a new bridge to get to town quicker, to shorten school bus routes. Nobody answered our letters. So then the Engineer said OK, you guys make phone calls. We did that. Finally, the County Engineer called me and said the State of Minnesota had called him to tell me to 'Call off your dogs! You'll get your bridge!' And we did."

Willard's ingenuity, versatility, and persistence underscores recent findings by rural sociologists and economists who find rural entrepreneurs and businesses more durable than urban businesses. Perhaps those urban planners in Fargo who have recently named themselves "Misfits," who welcome tinkerers and inventors and outsiders of all kinds will also welcome some rural types into their midst. And perhaps the US Army Corps of Engineers, now busy bulldozing away for the Dakota Access Pipeline, will stop and think, and listen to the undercurrents of their actions on the land and in the waters. It's political.

The FM diversion project broke ground on Monday, April 17, 2017. The officials leading the project chose this day to officially commemorate the twentieth anniversary of the 1997 flood.

911 Call

Woman with No Car

April 18th, 1997, 8:46 pm
Call 680
Abstract by Samantha Criswell
Quality assurance by Matthew Nelson.

Audio link: https://perma.cc/TN64-3BXZ

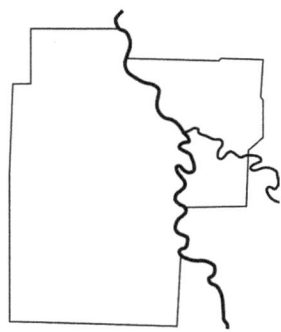

April 18th, 1997, 8:20 pm: Central Park has filled up.

Dispatcher: Alright, thanks for holding, can I help you?
Woman (panicked): Yes, I don't know where to go. We need to evacuate…
Dispatcher: Okay, okay. Um…
Woman: It's already started off by Cherry Street…um
Dispatcher: Okay, do you have a way to get out? Do you have a car?
Woman: No, we have no car. It broke down, something in the fuse.
Dispatcher: Okay, were you talking to somebody already?
Woman: Yeah, the guy told me to hold on.
(voices in background)
Dispatcher: Okay, and you're at…what's your address?
Woman: I'm at 633 4th Avenue South…there's a guy walking to Leevers to get some food because our car's been out. We've been trying to wait until, you know…
Dispatcher: Just a second…633 4th Avenue South?
Woman: Yeah…
Dispatcher: Yeah, 633 4th Avenue South. Okay, we're gonna get National Guard to come over there, okay? So he's heading to

Leevers, he's going in the right direction, okay? There are officers that'll help evacuate people if it gets that far, and they'll take you, okay?

Woman: Where are we gonna go?

Dispatcher: They're gonna take you to Red River High School, which is a shelter right now. Okay?

Woman: Wait…is…is there a phone there to contact…?

Dispatcher: Yep, there, there's phones there and everything, okay? The Red Cross is set up there and the Salvation Army, okay? We'll send someone over to 633 4th Avenue South, okay?

Woman: We're waiting for him to get back? We can't leave him.

Dispatcher: Okay..um…

Woman: And we have a dog!

Dispatcher: Okay you can bring your dog with you. Um, as far as him, if they are there before he gets back, go ahead and go with them to get out of the area because he's in Leevers, he's in a drier area, okay? They have not evacuated that yet.

Woman (stuttering): Okay, have they—I wanna make sure – did I hear…[unintelligible] Are we evacuated? I don't know, because they said 4th the one time they called, but they didn't say anything…

Dispatcher: We're starting at 4th Avenue South…let's see… you're gonna wanna get out 0-200 blocks. We're gonna get to your area here shortly. They evacuate also…

Woman: You are?

Dispatcher: Yep, because the water's coming that way.

Woman: Wha—

Dispatcher: Okay? So I'm gonna, we'll get a National Guard truck over there to help pick you up and take you over, um, out of the water. Okay?

Woman: Alright, thank you!

Dispatcher: Yep.

Woman: Bye.

4

Town and Gown: The University during and after Crisis

Document:

The University of North Dakota Flood Timeline

From *The Return of Lake Agassiz (1998)*

This is a hand-corrected draft of a timeline chronicling how the campus was impacted by the flood. The corrections are in the hand of long-time University of North Dakota employee, Jan Orvik. As Reuter notes in her foreword included above the University and the North Dakota Museum of Art are located at about 54 feet and thus escaped the worst damage. This timeline, however, speaks to just how much damage occurred nevertheless

Reference:
OGL #1351, Box 3, Folder 58. Elwyn B. Robinson Department of Special Collections, Chester Fritz Library, University of North Dakota, Grand Forks.

UNIVERSITY OF NORTH DAKOTA FLOOD TIMELINE

1996

Saturday, Oct. 26
-- Heavy rain and lightning delay Fighting Sioux/University of South Dakota football game. Rain saturates ground, setting stage for future flooding.

Nov. 16-17
-- Blizzard Andy strikes. Two members of the University die in the storm.

Dec. 16-18
-- Blizzard Betty hits.

Dec. 20
-- Blizzard Christopher.

1997

Jan. 9-11
-- Blizzard Elmo.

Jan. 22-23
-- Blizzard Franzi.

March 1
-- National Weather Service issues first flood forecast, predicting a record 49-foot flood.

March 3-4
-- Blizzard Gust.

March 4
-- Grand Forks City Council declares flood emergency.

March 15
-- Grand Forks and East Grand Forks opened Sandbag Central.
-- The two cities began raising dikes to 52 feet.

March 22
-- Women's basketball team wins national Division II NCAA Championship for first time.

March 29
-- Men's hockey team wins NCAA Division I Championship for sixth time.

April 1

-- Emergency Operations Center (EOC) opens to public.
-- Mayor Pat Owens declares Fighting Sioux/UND Day; champions in women's basketball, hockey, swimming, track and wrestling are honored.
-- Red River: 17.05 feet (Note: All readings taken at 9 pm unless otherwise noted)

April 4
-- Rodney Slater, U.S. Secretary of Transportation, visited North Dakota.
-- Students and staff volunteered to aid in diking.
April 5-7: Ice storm; Blizzard Hannah. Most of Red River Valley lost power.
-- KCNN Radio became the "voice of the blizzard," teaming with UND's radio station to broadcast news.
-- Red River: 27.55 feet (Flood stage: 28 feet)

April 7
-- At 9 p.m., Red River level was at 37.49 feet.
-- Red River: 37.49 feet

Thursday, April 10
-- Red River rose to 41.21 feet.

Friday, April 11
-- Parts of I-29 between Fargo and Grand Forks are closed because of water.
-- Students asked to help residents build private dikes as well as work at Sandbag Central.
-- UND Smith Hall Cafeteria closed to allow construction of clay dike.
-- Clay dikes in cities now at 52-foot level.
-- National Weather Service predicted crest of 49 feet would occur between April 20 and 27.
-- Red River at 42.48 feet. 17

Saturday, April 12
-- Vice President Al Gore visited Fargo and Breckenridge to view flooding.
-- Red River: 42.63 feet

Sunday, April 13
-- Residents began building sandbag dikes in the Point area of East Grand Fokrs.
-- Grand Forks officials began putting together and evacuation plan.
-- Red River at 43.22 feet. 37

Monday, April 14
-- Dike patrols begin.
-- Red River: 44.69 feet

Tuesday, April 15
-- Point and Sorlie Bridges bettween Grand Forks and East Grand Forks are closed.
-- National Weather Service raises crest prediction from 49 to 50 feet.
-- University Avenue underpass goes under water.
-- Red River: 46.79

Wednesday, April 16
-- I-29 closed between Grafton and Grand Forks.
-- Gateway Drive and parts of 32nd Ave. S. went under water.
-- About 400 East Grand Forks residents were evacuated.

-- At 2 p.m., President Baker canceled classes for the remainder of the afternoon and Thursday to free students, faculty and staff for the flood fight. The University remained open to respond to the flood effort.
-- Grand Forks residents summoned to evacuation meetings.
-- National Weather Service issued a new flood crest prediction of 50.5 feet.
-- Red River at 48.98 feet, a new record.

Thursday, April 17
-- UND removed hazardous wastes from areas that could be flooded.
-- Cracks appeared in Lincoln Park dike.
-- Cracks in dikes prompted evacuation of Griggs Park and Sherlock Park in East Grand Forks.
-- Grand Forks residents near the river were advised to evacuate.
-- National Weather Service raised crest predition to 52 feet.
-- At midnight, Red River was at 51.28 feet. (50.98 feet @ 9 pm)

Friday, April 18
-- Lincoln Park and Lincoln Drive evacuated. Soon after, Riverside, Central Park, belmont Road, Cottonwood and Chestnut Street areas were also evacuated.
-- At 2:45 a.m., Red River at 51.42 feet. At noon, it stood at 52.19 feet.
-- National Weather Service revised crest prediction to 53 feet.
-- UND cancelled classes to allow University Community members to volunteer.
-- Point area of East Grand Forks went under water.
-- At UND, residence hall parking lots began flooding. Students encouraged to evacuate.
-- Lincoln Drive neighborhood went under water by 4:30 p.m.
-- The Kennedy Bridge closed.
-- Red River at 52.6 feet at 8 p.m.
-- National Weather Service raised crest prediction to 54 feet.
-- Water restrictions imposed as sweage lift stations failed.
-- Emergency Operations Center moved to UND campus. Overnight, the campus would also house the Naitonal Guard, U.S. Army Corps of Engineers, Coast Guard, City Engineer's Office, City and State Health Departmetns, Fire Department, Police Department, and, temporarily, the Grand Forks Herald and the Mayor's Office.
-- UND battles to save Smith Hall.
-- City lost water plant.
-- At 11 p.m., a dike near the Kennedy Bridge in East Grand Forks failed, flooding Sherlock Park.
-- Red River at 53.02 feet at midnight. (52.91 feet @ 9pm)

Saturday, April 19
-- Evacuation mandatory for all Grand Forks residents within the 100-year flood plain.
-- Gov. Schafer remained in city to work with city officials.
-- Fight to save Smith Hall continues; had to be abandoned at 3:30 a.m.
-- Diking efforts are abandoned as more evacuations are ordered.
-- Red River High School becomes evacuation destination; later, evacuees are sent to Grand Forks Air Force Base.
-- At 4 a.m., North Dakota Unviersity System Chancellor Larry Isak is roused by the State

Disaster Emergency Management Team and told about the situation in Grand Forks. He arranged for Grand Forks evacuees to be housed at the Valley City State University Mayvill State University, and UND-Lake Region.
-- After learning that the Water Plant had failed, President Baker canceled classes for the remainder of the semester and asked students to leave the city.
-- UND officials began meeting to determine how best to save the University from flooding.
-- The University became flood-fighting headquarters for University, city, state, and national agencies.
-- UND's steam plant failed, causing evacuation of the medical park.
-- Preparations began to move the University's mainframe computer to Fargo. The computer was vital to keep remaining NDUS functions running and to pay staff and faculty on all 11 campuses.
-- Sometime after 4 p.m., fire was discovered downtown. It would eventually burn 11 buildings before being brought under control.
-- Wilkerson and the Medical School Complex were inundated by raw sewage after lift stations failed.
-- Red River : 53.58 feet

Sunday, April 20
-- Evacuations continue.
-- Fourteen people remained on campus to save what could be saved. The first of twice-daily meetings began. Saving communication systems was a priority.
-- First Lady Toby Baker went on KCNN Radio to request volunteers to help save items in the Chester Fritz Library.
-- Medical faculty organized to preserve research and lab animals.
-- The fire continued downtown; three private homes burned. Electric power was shut off in most of the city.
-- Ryan Hall on campus became the headquarters for national and state media.
-- People in the city of Thompson offered food, showers and a place to sleep.
-- The Aerospace Network accomodated FEMA and television media.
-- By the end of the day, three-fourths of Grand Forks and all of East Grand Forks had been evacuated.
-- Red River at just over 54 feet at 6 p.m., reached 54.19 feet at midnight.

Monday, April 21
-- Water threatened a transformer near the Hughes Fine Arts Center. University staff, National Guard, Air Force Base personnel, firemen, EOC staff, and others worked through the night to sandbag the transformer, the last communication link left in the city besides the besieged US West workers downtown.
-- The University began formulating plans to begin a phone bank to maintain contact with students, faculty and staff.
-- The Energy and Environmental Research Center had to be shut down because of flooding.
-- UND's Student Health team was asked to go downtown to give tetanus shots to US West and NSP workers, firefighters, National Guardsmen and others.
-- UND housed and maintained Department of Transportation trucks after their facility went down.
-- Chancellor Larry Isaak toured flooded areas by helicopter.

-- President Baker announced that UND would hold Summer School on time, beginning May 12.
-- Plans were formulated to begin a "Virtual University."
-- Red River: 54.29 feet

Tuesday, April 22
-- President Clinton visited the flooded cities, and ordered FEMA to pay 100 percent, rather than 75 percent, of immediate emergency work. UND aided the Air Force Base in hosting the visit.
-- National Guard troops worked into the night to sandbag a Northern States Power electrical switching station to provide power. US West employees continued their fight to protect a telephone cable vault in the basement of their flooded downtown building.
-- Enrollment Services mailed newsletters from Mayville and set up an office in the Rural Technology Center.
-- UND, city, state and national officials began discussing the possibility of using UND residence halls to house members of the community.
-- Bob Boyd (Continuing Education) was named chair of the UND Transition Task Force to oversee UND's flood recovery. The goal was to operate a Virtual University by April 28.
-- UND's mainframe computer was installed at NDSU and run by UND staff members.
-- Grand Forks county offices temporarily located in Larimore.
-- Red River: Crested at midnight, 54.33 feet; 9 p.m. 53.78 feet

Wednesday, April 23
-- This was the first day that the river began falling, to 54.06 feet.
-- American Red Cross President Elizabeth Dole and North Dakota First Lady Nancy Schafer toured flooded areas with Mayor Owens.
-- University began figuring out how to clean flooded buildings.
-- Red Tag Diner opened.
-- A Volunteer Center was set up, allowing people to call in for information. It handled more than 2,000 calls each day.
-- UND's academic deans met for the first time since the flood.
-- Red River: 52.9'

Thursday, April 24
-- Some Grand Forks residents were allowed to visit their homes for a few hours.
-- Presdient Baker attended the State Board of Higher Education board meeting in Bismarck.
-- 51.68

Friday, April 25
-- Newt Gingrich, Speaker of the U.S. House of Representatives, visited the cities.
-- Minnesota higher education officials held a press conference in Grand Forks, at which President Baker presided.
-- 50.35

Saturday, April 26
-- More neighborhoods were opened.
-- 48.81

Sunday, April 27
-- I-29 was reopened between Fargo and Grand Forks.
-- 47.39

Monday, April 28
-- Kennedy Bridge between Grand Forks and East Grand Forks was opened.

-- The Grand Forks City Council met for the first time since the flood.
-- UND began housing volunteers in residence halls and Hyslop Sports Center.
-- U.S. Congressman and House Majority Leader Richard Armey, a native of Cando and alumnus of UND, visited the campus and city.
-- UND allowed students in family housing to return home.
-- Students in residence halls west of the English Coulee were asked to return to pick up possessions.

Tuesday, April 29
-- Some University buildings were opened, and UND began pumping water out of buildings.
-- An anonymous "angel" announced donations of $2,000 to flood victims.

Wednesday, April 30
-- UND held anInteractive Town Meeting, with satellite feeds across the state and Minnesota.

Thursday, May 1
-- Cleanup began in the cities, and berms overflowed with ruined possessions.
-- Remaining UND students were allowed into residence halls to retrieve their belongings.
-- United Hospital's emergency room opened. Water was supplied tby the National Guard.

Friday, May 2
-- Water was restored to most of Grand Forks. Residents were asked to boil the water before using it to cook, drink or wash.
-- President Baker announced that UND would provide temporary housing to faculty, staff and community members.

Saturday, May 3
-- Water service was restored to the area west of the English Coulee.
-- Cleaning contracts were awarded at the University.
-- UND assigned space in the Rural Technology Center and the Law School to displaced businesses.

Sunday, May 4
-- North Dakota's Congressional Delegation asks the National Weather Service and the Army Corps of Engineers to explain why they did not share information that could have given a more accurate flood crest forecast.

Monday, May 5
-- Workers began removing temporary dikes.
-- Damages to public buildings were assessed. At UND, 72 of the 238 buildings on campus were damaged.

Thursday, May 9
-- UND officially re-opened.
-- The last flood evacuees left the Grand Forks Air Force Base.

-- UND's Steam Plant was restored, making heat and water available to some buildings.
-- President Baker opened the Hyslop Sports Center shower facilities to the Grand Forks community, since few people had running water, hot water, or electricity in their homes.

Saturday, May 10
-- University and Grand Forks community members began checking into UND residence halls.

Monday, May 12
-- Summer Session begins at UND, on time.
-- University Children's Center reopens, offering free child care.
-- City water is declared drinkable by city officials.
-- The UND Foundation launched a nationwide UND flood Recovery fund drive to raise money for the University's recovery.

Wednesday, May 14
-- FEMA director James Lee Witt toured the area to assess damages.
-- President Baker addressed faculty and staff in a standing-room only briefing.
-- An Off-Campus Housing office was formed to aid students in their search for housing.
-- Hyslop Sports Center began hosting flood recovery volunteers

Thursday, May 15
-- Mayor Owens met with First Lady Hillary Clinton and President Clinton to discuss the need for the federal disaster aid bill, which was being held up by Congress.

Saturday, May 17
-- UND's mainframe comaputer was moved from NDSU back "home" to UND.
-- The Sorlie Bridge on DeMers Avenue reopened.

Monday, May 19
-- The Medical School reopened.
-- River Falls below flood stage

Friday, May 23
-- The cities celebrated their survival at a free barbecue at Memorial Stadium, sponsored by area businesses and "Texas Lil, owner of a dude ranch in Texas.

June, 1997
-- UND's radio station, KFJM-FM, went back on the air. The other two stations were not yet restored.
-- The flooded eroded Summer School and fall registration. An intense enrollment campaign began.
-- More than 90 million pounds of flood debris had been hauled to landfills.
-- The flood disaster relief bill was finally signed June 13, after being held up for weeks of Congressional wrangling.
-- On June 18, 700 children were evacuated from Kelly and Agassiz schools after black fungus mold was discovered in tunnels and crawl spaces.
-- The Bouncin' Back Bash was held Sunday, June 22, at the Memorial Stadium.

-- UND housed 38 displaced businesses.

August 26
UND's fall semester began on time, with a final enrollment of 10,395 studetns, down from last year's total of 11,300.

Flood Gauge Readings

Records of flooding on the Red River of the North have been kept since 1882 by the U.S. Geological Survey. The gauge, which has been moved several times over the years, is now located at River Mile 297.6, just south of the Sorlie Bridge on DeMers Avenue. The bottom of the river channel at the location is River Gauge 0.0, or 779.0 feet above mean sea level. Flood stage in Grand Forks is 28 feet. During the 1997 event, the Red River passed above flood stage in the late evening hours of Friday, April 4, and did not fall below 28 feet until Monday, May 19. The following table of gauge readings was provided by Dr. Paul Todhunter of the UND Department of Geography.

Tuesday, April 1

Midnight	16.95 feet
3 a.m.	16.98 feet
6 a.m.	16.96 feet
9 a.m.	16.97 feet
Noon	17.02 feet
3 p.m.	16.98 feet
6 p.m.	17.02 feet
9 p.m.	17.05 feet

Wednesday, April 2

Midnight	17.08 feet
3 a.m.	17.10 feet
6 a.m.	17.13 feet
9 a.m.	17.15 feet
Noon	17.20 feet
3 p.m.	17.29 feet
6 p.m.	17.40 feet
9 p.m.	17.55 feet

Thursday, April 3

Midnight	17.75 feet
3 a.m.	17.93 feet
6 a.m.	18.11 feet
9 a.m.	18.34 feet
Noon	18.78 feet
3 p.m.	19.36 feet
6 p.m.	20.14 feet
9 p.m.	21.02 feet

Friday, April 4

Midnight	21.90 feet
3 a.m.	22.83 feet
6 a.m.	23.69 feet
9 a.m.	24.50 feet
Noon	25.27 feet
3 p.m.	25.98 feet
6 p.m.	26.77 feet
9 p.m.	27.55 feet

Saturday, April 5

Midnight	28.31 feet
3 a.m.	28.80 feet
6 a.m.	27.90 feet
9 a.m.	26.32 feet
Noon	31.49 feet
3 p.m.	31.89 feet
6 p.m.	32.79 feet
9 p.m.	33.07 feet

Sunday, April 6

Midnight	33.34 feet
3 a.m.	33.62 feet
6 a.m.	33.89 feet
9 a.m.	34.17 feet
Noon	34.45 feet
3 p.m.	34.72 feet
6 p.m.	35.00 feet
9 p.m.	35.28 feet

Monday, April 7

Midnight	35.55 feet
3 a.m.	35.83 feet
6 a.m.	36.10 feet
9 a.m.	36.38 feet
Noon	36.66 feet
3 p.m.	36.93 feet
6 p.m.	37.21 feet
9 p.m.	37.49 feet

Tuesday, April 8

Midnight	37.76 feet
3 a.m.	38.04 feet
6 a.m.	38.31 feet
9 a.m.	38.59 feet
Noon	38.87 feet
3 p.m.	39.14 feet
6 p.m.	39.42 feet
9 p.m.	39.70 feet

Wednesday, April 9

Midnight	39.97 feet
3 a.m.	40.25 feet
6 a.m.	40.52 feet
9 a.m.	40.80 feet
Noon	40.85 feet
3 p.m.	41.00 feet
6 p.m.	41.20 feet
9 p.m.	41.30 feet

Thursday, April 10

Midnight	41.39 feet
3 a.m.	41.51 feet
6 a.m.	41.54 feet
9 a.m.	41.62 feet
Noon	41.66 feet
3 p.m.	41.73 feet
6 p.m.	41.77 feet
9 p.m.	41.81 feet

Friday, April 11

Midnight	41.85 feet
3 a.m.	41.87 feet
6 a.m.	41.95 feet
9 a.m.	41.99 feet
Noon	42.03 feet
3 p.m.	42.07 feet
6 p.m.	42.12 feet
9 p.m.	42.17 feet

Saturday, April 12

Midnight	42.25 feet
3 a.m.	42.28 feet
6 a.m.	42.29 feet
9 a.m.	42.36 feet
Noon	42.42 feet
3 p.m.	42.47 feet
6 p.m.	42.55 feet
9 p.m.	42.63 feet

Sunday, April 13

Midnight	42.71 feet
3 a.m.	42.77 feet
6 a.m.	42.85 feet
9 a.m.	42.94 feet
Noon	43.12 feet
3 p.m.	43.14 feet
6 p.m.	43.27 feet
9 p.m.	43.37 feet

Monday, April 14

Midnight	43.53 feet
3 a.m.	43.66 feet
6 a.m.	43.78 feet
9 a.m.	43.92 feet
Noon	44.08 feet
3 p.m.	44.31 feet
6 p.m.	44.52 feet
9 p.m.	44.69 feet

Tuesday, April 15

Midnight	44.93 feet
3 a.m.	45.23 feet
6 a.m.	45.44 feet
9 a.m.	45.70 feet
Noon	45.96 feet
3 p.m.	46.19 feet
6 p.m.	46.47 feet
9 p.m.	46.79 feet

Wednesday, April 16

Midnight	47.10 feet
3 a.m.	47.43 feet
6 a.m.	47.66 feet
9 a.m.	47.96 feet
Noon	48.28 feet
3 p.m.	48.53 feet
6 p.m.	48.72 feet
9 p.m.	48.98 feet

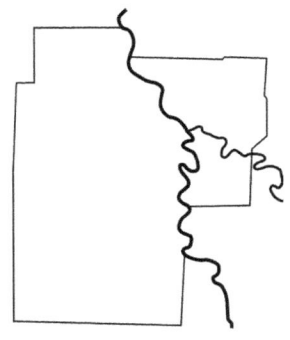

Document:
Flood Gauge Readings

From *The Return of Lake Agassiz (1998)*

Records of flooding on the Red River of the North have been kept since 1882 by the U.S. Geological Survey. The gauge, which has been moved several times over the years, is now located at Mile 297 .6, just south of the Sorlie Bridge on DeMers Avenue. The bottom of the river channel at the location is River Gauge 0.0, or 779.0 feet above mean sea level. Flood stage in Grand Forks is 28 feet. During the 1997 event, the Red River passed above flood stage in the late evening hours of Friday, April 4, and did not fall below 28 feet until Monday, May 19. The following table of gauge readings was provided by Dr. Paul Todhunter of the UND Department of Geography.

Tuesday, April 1
Midnight.........16.95 feet
3 a.m................16.96 feet
6 a.m................16.96 feet
9 a.m................16.97 feet
Noon...............17.02 feet
3 p.m. ....16.98 feet
6 p.m. ....17.02 feet
9 p.m. ....17.05 feet

Wednesday, April 2
Midnight ....17.08 feet
3 a.m. ....17.10 feet
6 a.m. ....17.13 feet
9 a.m. ....17.15 feet
Noon ....17.20 feet
3 p.m. ....17.29 feet
6 p.m. ....17.40 feet
9 p.m. ....17.55 feet

Thursday, April 3
Midnight.........17.75 feet
3 a.m. ....17.93 feet
6 a.m................18.11 feet
9 a.m................18.34 feet
Noon...............18.78 feet
3 p.m. ....19.36 feet
6 p.m. ....20.14 feet
9 p.m. ....21.02 feet

Friday, April 4
Midnight.........21.90 feet
3 a.m. ....22.83 feet
6 a.m. ....23.69 feet
9 a.m. ....24.50 feet
Noon ....25.27 feet
3 p.m. ....25.98 feet
6 p.m. ....26.77 feet
9 p.m. ....27.55 feet

Saturday, April 5
Midnight ....28.31 feet
3 a.m. ....28.80 feet
6 a.m. ....27.90 feet
9 a.m. ....26.32 feet
Noon ....31.49 feet
3 p.m. ....31.89 feet
6 p.m. ....32.79 feet
9 p.m. ....33.07 feet

Sunday, April 6
Midnight.........33.34 feet
3 a.m.................33.62 feet
6 a.m.................33.89 feet
9 a.m.................34.17 feet
Noon................34.45 feet
3 p.m. ....34.72 feet
6 p.m. ....35.00 feet
9 p.m. ....35.28 feet

Monday, April 7
Midnight ....35.55 feet
3 a.m. ....35.83 feet
6 a.m. ....36.10 feet
9 a.m. ....36.38 feet
Noon ....36.66 feet
3 p.m. ....36.93 feet
6 p.m. ....37.21 feet
9 p.m. ....37.49 feet

Tuesday, April 8
Midnight ....37.76 feet
3 a.m. ....38.04 feet
6 a.m. ....38.31 feet
9 a.m. ....38.59 feet
Noon ....38.87 feet
3 p.m. ....39.14 feet
6 p.m. ....39.42 feet
9 p.m. ....39.70 feet

Wednesday, April 9
Midnight.........39.97 feet
3 a.m.................40.25 feet
6 a.m.................40.52 feet
9 a.m.................40.80 feet
Noon................40.85 feet
3 p.m. ....41.00 feet
6 p.m. ....41.20 feet
9 p.m. ....41.30 feet

Thursday, April 10
Midnight ....41.39 feet
3 a.m. ....41.51 feet
6 a.m. ....41.54 feet
9 a.m. ....41.62 feet
Noon ....41.66 feet
3 p.m. .... 41.73 feet
6 p.m. ....41.77 feet
9 p.m. ....41.81 feet

Friday, April 11
Midnight.........41.85 feet
3 a.m................41.87 feet
6 a.m................41.95 feet
9 a.m................41.99 feet
Noon...............42.03 feet
3 p.m. ....42.07 feet
6 p.m. ....42.12 feet
9 p.m. ....42.17 feet

Saturday, April 12
Midnight.........42.25 feet
3 a.m................42.28 feet
6 a.m................42.29 feet
9 a.m................42.36 feet
Noon...............42.42 feet
3 p.m. ....42.47 feet
6 p.m. ....42.55 feet
9 p.m. ....42.63 feet

Sunday, April 13
Midnight ....42.71 feet
3 a.m. ....42.77 feet
6 a.m. ....42.85 feet
9 a.m. ....42.94 feet
Noon ....43.12 feet
3 p.m. ....43.14 feet
6 p.m. ....43.27 feet
9 p.m. ....43.37 feet

Monday, April 14
Midnight ....43.53 feet
3 a.m. ....43.66 feet
6 a.m. ....43.78 feet
9 a.m. ....43.92 feet
Noon ....44.08 feet
3 p.m. ....44.31 feet
6 p.m. ....44.52 feet
9 p.m. ....44.69 feet

Tuesday, April 15
Midnight.........44.93 feet
3 a.m................45.23 feet
6 a.m................45.44 feet
9 a.m................45.70 feet
Noon...............45.96 feet
3 p.m. ....46.19 feet
6 p.m. ....46.47 feet
9 p.m. ....46.79 feet

Wednesday, April 16
Midnight ....47.10 feet
3 a.m. ....47.43 feet
6 a.m. ....47.66 feet
9 a.m. ....47.96 feet
Noon ....48.28 feet
3 p.m. ....48.53 feet
6 p.m. ....48.72 feet
9 p.m. ....48.98 feet

Thursday, April 17
Midnight ....49.19 feet
3 a.m. ....49.43 feet
6 a.m. ....49.70 feet
9 a.m. ....49.97 feet
Noon ....50.24 feet
3 p.m. ....50.47 feet
6 p.m. ....50.75 feet
9 p.m. ....50.98 feet

Friday, April 18
Midnight......... 51.28 feet
3 a.m. ....51.58 feet
6 a.m. ....51.96 feet
9 a.m. ....52.27 feet
Noon ....52.49 feet
3 p.m. ....52.65 feet
6 p.m. .... 52.75 feet
9 p.m. ....52.91 feet

Saturday, April 19
Midnight ....53.02 feet
3 a.m. ....52.97 feet
6 a.m. ....53.10 feet
9 a.m. ....53.16 feet
Noon ....53.21 feet
3 p.m. ....53.39 feet
6 p.m. ....53.50 feet
9 p.m. ....53.58 feet

Sunday, April 20
Midnight ....53.65 feet
3 a.m. ....53.71 feet
6 a.m. ....53.78 feet
9 a.m. ....53.82 feet
Noon ....53.88 feet
3 p.m. ....53.91 feet
6 p.m. ....54.01 feet
9 p.m. ....53.90 feet

Monday, April 21
Midnight ....54.19 feet
3 a.m. ....53.90 feet
6 a.m................ 53.98 feet
9 a.m. ....54.08 feet
Noon ....54.18 feet
3 p.m. ....54.23 feet
6 p.m. ....54.26 feet
9 p.m. ....54.29 feet

Tuesday, April 22
Midnight ....54.33 feet
3 a.m. ....54.30 feet
6 a.m. ....54.11 feet
9 a.m. ....54.06 feet
Noon ....54.04 feet
3 p.m. ....53.89 feet
6 p.m. ....53.83 feet
9 p.m. ....53.78 feet

Wednesday, April 23
Midnight......... 53.69 feet
3 a.m. ....53.59 feet
6 a.m. ....53.50 feet
9 a.m. ....53.43 feet
Noon ....53.31 feet
3 p.m. ....53.13 feet
6 p.m. ....52.98 feet
9 p.m. ....52.90 feet

Thursday, April 24
Midnight ....52.85 feet
3 a.m. ....52.69 feet
6 a.m. ....52.60 feet
9 a.m. ....52.43 feet
Noon ....52.34 feet
3 p.m. ....52.25 feet
6 p.m. ....51.95 feet
9 p.m. ....51.68 feet

Thursday, April 24
Midnight ....52.85 feet
3 a.m. ....52.69 feet
6 a.m...............52.60 feet
9 a.m...............52.43 feet
Noon ....52.34 feet
3 p.m. ....52.25 feet
6 p.m. ....51.95 feet
9 p.m. ....51.68 feet

Friday, April 25
Midnight ....51.47 feet
3 a.m. ....51.28 feet
6 a.m. ....51.09 feet
9 a.m. ....50.90 feet
Noon ....50.83 feet
3 p.m. ....50.74 feet
6 p.m. ....50.58 feet
9 p.m. ....50.35 feet

Saturday, April 26
Midnight ....50.13 feet
3 a.m. ....49.94 feet
6 a.m. ....49.76 feet
9 a.m. ....49.54 feet
Noon ....49.34 feet
3 p.m. ....49.17 feet
6 p.m. ....49.01 feet
9 p.m. ....48.81 feet

Sunday, April 27
Midnight ....48.62 feet
3 a.m. ....48.36 feet
6 a.m. ....47.67 feet
9 a.m. ....48.01 feet
Noon ....47.82 feet
3 p.m. ....47.64 feet
6 p.m. ....47.52 feet
9 p.m. ....47.39 feet

Monday, April 28
Midnight ....46.91 feet
3 a.m. ....46.81 feet
6 a.m. ....46.89 feet
9 a.m. ....46.59 feet
Noon ....46.62 feet
3 p.m. ....46.58 feet
6 p.m. ....46.31 feet
9 p.m. ....46.27 feet

Tuesday, April 29
Midnight ....45.98 feet
3 a.m. ....45.84 feet
6 a.m. ....45.69 feet
9 a.m. ....45.55 feet
Noon ....45.40 feet
3 p.m. ....45.39 feet
6 p.m. ....45.28 feet
9 p.m. ....45.17 feet

Wednesday, April 30
Midnight......... 45.06 feet
3 a.m. ....44.96 feet
6 a.m. ....44.83 feet
9 a.m. ....44.72 feet
Noon ....44.57 feet
3 p.m. ....44.46 feet
6 p.m. ....44.35 feet
9 p.m. ....44.26 feet

Thursday, May 1
Midnight ....44.13 feet

"Libraries Lost"
Jennifer Ring from *Under the Whelming Tide* (1998)

Jennifer Ring, LIBRARIES LOST. Grand Forks is the home of the University of North Dakota, and consequently scholars, writers, teachers, and students. During the flood whole libraries were lost, many of them irreplaceable. This berm is piled with the collection of Audrey Henderson-Nocho and included signed first editions of African-American authors and historical legal texts.

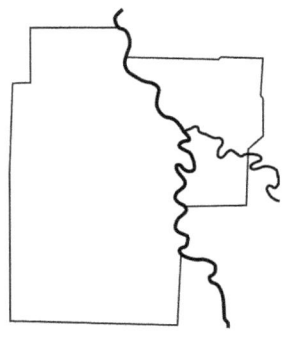

Document:

Books Lost in the Flood

This is an early draft of the books lost during the flood dating to September 9, 1997. It's particularly interesting to see the wide range of subjects: from books on yoga, to real estate, home furnishings, to teaching swimming; one wonders if the teachings of any of these books came in handy during the flood and its recovery or if their knowledge was lost along with the physical containers.

Reference:
OGL #1351, Box 7, Folder 65. September 9, 1997. Elwyn B. Robinson Department of Special Collections, Chester Fritz Library, University of North Dakota, Grand Forks.

Books Lost in Flood

This is a preliminary list of books lost in the flood. As the library is notified about additional losses, these books will be added to the list. If you are interested in replacing any of these titles, please contact Cynthia Shabb at (701) 777-4623 or cshabb@plains.nodak.edu.

Last updated: August 1, 1997

FLOOD LOSS -- MONOGRAPHS		
Call Number	**Title**	**Author/ Editor**
F R578b 1992	A break with charity	Rinaldi, Ann
970.04 G816p 1995	A pioneer sampler	Greenwood, Barbara
LB 2331 .F74 1979	Academic Culture and Faculty Development	Freedman, Marvin G.
HQ784.T4 K37 1979	ACT guide to children's television	Kaye, Evelyn
RA 644 .A25 A45 1990	Adolescents in the AIDS epidemic	Gardner, William, et al
TD 427 .O7...	Advances in the identification & analysis of organic pollutants v.2	Keith, Lawrence H.
N6538.N5 F56 1973	Afro-American artist	Fine, Elsa Honig
P96 .P75 K39 1993	Age of manipulation:	Key, Wilson Bryan
RA 644 . A25 A36353 1989	AIDS in an aging society	Riley, Matilda White
E528.5 2nd R46 1991	All for the Union	Rhodes, Elisha Hunt
NK4005 .H45 1970	American art pottery	Henzke, Lucile
HC 106.6 .C317 1971	American economy in conflict	Carson, Robert Barry
JK 1764 .L43 1976	American institutions, political opinion, and public policy	Lehnen, Robert G.
QL 805.H64 1982	Analysis of vertebrate structure	Hildebrand, Milton
PS591.N4 W5 1924x	Anthology of verse by American Negroes	White, Newman Ivey
BL2600 .B8 1970	Anthropology and religion	Buck, Peter Henry, Sir
GN27 .M37 1974	Anthropology through science fiction	Mason, Carol
TD 180 .A38 V 22	Aquatic toxicology and water quality management	Nriagu, Jerome D., et al
NA680 .J5713 1969	Architecture since 1945	Joedicke, Jurgen
NA680 .J448 1982	Architecture today	Jencks, Charles
N 72 G68 1961	Art and culture: critical essays	Greenberg, Clement
TT270 .B57 1985	Art of decorative stenciling	Bishop, Adele
N 71 .A7475 1991	Art theory and criticism: an anthology of farmalist, avant-garde, ...	Everett, Sally

Books Lost in   http://www.und.nodak.edu/dept/library/flood/floodbk.htm

Call Number	Title	Author
PS3513.I74 Z542 1977	As ever	Ginsberg, Allen
Q162 .A8 1984	Asimov's New guide to science	Asimov, Isaac
E185.97.D73 A3 1968	Autobiography of W. E. B. DuBois	Du Bois, W.E.B.
F 1246 .G36 1980	Baja California guidebook: a descriptive traveler's guide	Wheelock, Walt
ML286 .C48 1965	Ballad literature and popular music of the olden time	Chappell, William
TR287 .G74 1986	Basic darkroom book	Grimm, Tom
E470 .B344 1956	Battles and leaders of the Civil War	Johnson, Robert Underwood, et al
E470 .B346 1956	Battles and leaders of the civil war	Bradford, Ned
RC 489.B4...1981	Behavioral assessment: a practical handbook	Hersen, Michel
F1443 .B65 1986	Belize, a new nation in Central America	Bolland, O. Nigel
PN6111 .B47 1988	Best short plays	
PR6013.R349 B47 1912	Between two thieves	Dehan, Richard
JK 1967 .S55 1984	Beyond the electoral connection...	Mead, Lawrence M.
JK 1764 .M4 1986	Beyond entitlement: the social obligations of citizenship	Shienbaum, Kim Ezra
TD 423.D83 1972	Biochemical ecology of water pollution	Dugan, Patrick R.
QH 545.A1 M44 1972	Biology of pollution	Mellanby, Kenneth
RC1235 .B548 1989	Biomechanics of sport	Vaughan, Christopher L.
GR 735 .R68	Birds with human souls: a guide to bird symbolism	Rowland, Beryl
BT 734.2.c6 1969	Black theology and black power	Cone, James H.
PR 4148 .B52... 1990	Blake and his bibles	Erdman, David V.
PR. 4147 .B5 1963	Blake's apocalypse: a study in poetic argument	Frye, Northrop
PR 4147 .C8 1973	Blake's sublime allegory...	Punter, David
PR 4148. P5 ...1982	Blake, Hegel and dialectic	Erdman, David V.
PR 4147 .E7 1954	Blake, prophet against empire: a poet's interp. of the history of his own times	Bloom, Harold
PR 4146. F7 1966	Blake: a collection of critical essays	Curran, Stuart
ND 553 .D774 T6 1976	Bride and the bachelors: five masters of the avant-garde	Tomkins, Calvin
NK4085 .C65	British art pottery	Coysh, Arthur Wilfred
PG 3326... 1976	Brothers Karamazov	Dostoyevsky, Fyodor
PG 3328 .Z7 1985	Burden of vision: Dostoevsky's spiritual art	Panichas, George Andrew
HF 5415 .122 .S72 1991	Careers in marketing	Stair, Lila B.
HV 91 .G58 1983	Causes and cures of welfare: new evidence on the social psychology	Goodwin, Leonard

RA 644.A25 K44 1995	Changing HIV risk behavior: practial strategies	Kelly, Jeffrey A.
BS2505 .J4 1923	Character of Paul	Jefferson, Charles Edward
DS 753 .C533	Chinese government in Ming times	Grimm, Tilemann
B 125 .E25 1967	Chinese mind: essentials of Chinese Philosophy	East-West Philosophers' Conference
FINE ARTS M25.B3 B8x 1896	Chromatic fantasy and fugue	Bach, Johann Sebastian
TR 850 .M276	Cinematography: a guide for film makers and film teachers	Malkiewicz, J. Kris
Jf 493 .U6 S36 1989	Citizen lawmakers: the ballot initiative revolution	Schmidt, David D.
JK 1764 .C525 1987	Citizen participation in public decision making	DeSario, Jack, et al
F391 .G68 1991	Claiming their land	Gould, Florence C.
F1435 .C6 1973	Classic Maya collapse	Culbert, T. Patrick
PN183 .K4 1980	Classical rhetoric and its Christian and secular tradition from ancient to modern times	Kennedy, George Alexander
QL737.C2 Y55 1951	Clever coyote	Young, Stanley Paul
Geology TN800 .M8 1968	Coal and coal-bearing strata	Murchison, Duncan, et al
Geology TN 800 .F7 1961	Coal: its formation and composition	Francis, Wilfrid
PG 3476 .P27...1977	Collected short prose...Boris Pasternak	Pasternak, Boris Leonidovich
LC212.862 C65 1996	Combatting sexual harassment in higher education	Lott, Bernice, et al
HQ782 .M325 1981	Come with us to playgroup	Magee, Patricia Boggia
HQ 76.25 .C66 1992	Coming out: an anthology of international gay and lesbian writings	Likosky, Stephan
HV 91.C4754 1980	Compassion and responsibility	Breul, Frank R., et al
HV5825 .C634 1993	Confronting drug policy	Bayer, Ronald, et al
B128.C8 S56 1973b	Confucius	Smith, David Howard
QL 737.C4 1980	Conservation and management of whales	Allen, Kenneth Radway
PR 4144.J43...1983	Continuing city: William Blake's Jerusalem	Paley, Morton D.
PR 4148.S95...1983	Conversing in paradise:poetic genius and identity as community in Blake's Los	Deen, Leonard W.
PN 1998.3 .C69 1990	Coppola	Cowie, Peter
E78.15 M63 1976	Corporation and the Indian	Miner, H. Craig
E98.F6 C83 1978	Coyote stories	Bright, William
PR9199.3.A8 D3 1993	Dancing girls and other stories	Atwood, Margaret Eleanor

PR590 .R27 1980	Dark interpreter	Rajan, Tilottama
PN 1998 .A3 L3792 1984	David Lean	Anderegg, Michael A.
HV5825 .D38 1987	Dealing with drugs	Hamowy, Ronald
E470 .M69 1955	Decisive battles of the Civil War	Mitchell, Joseph Brady
E 661 .M37 1986	Decline of popular politics	McGerr, Michael E.
TA683.2 .W48 1979	Design of concrete structures	Nilson, Arthur H.
LB1140.35 .C74 H47 1990	Designing creative materials for young children	Herr, Judy
PS3521.E735 D48 1990	Dharma bums	Kerouac, Jack
RC455.2C4 D54 1994	Diagnostic and statistical manual of mental disorders	American Psychiatric Association
ND 553.D774 C313 1971	Dialogues with Marcel Duchamp	Cabanne, Pierre
FINE ARTS MT872 .D43 1990	Diction for singers	Wall, Joan
Jf 493.U6 C76 1989	Direct democracy: the politics of initiative	Cronin, Thomas E.
PN 56 .L6 1986	Discourses of desire: gender, genre, and epistolary fictions	Kauffman, Linda S.
JF 493.U6 B5 1970	Documents on the state-wide initiative, referendum	Beard, Charles Austin
PG 3328...1962	Dostoevsky	Carr, Edward Halett
PG 3328 .G6613 1975	Dostoevsky: a biography	Grossman, Leonid Petrovich
PG 3328...1962	Dostoevsky: a self-portrait	Coulson, Jessie
RC1230 .W33 1989	Drugs and the athlete	Wadler, Gary I.
OVERSIZE NK2406 .E15 1983	Early American furniture, from settlement to city	Madigan, Mary Jean Smith, et al
HQ784.T4 L48 1988	Early Window	Liebert, Robert M.
HC79.E5 R52 1981	Ecodevelopment	Riddell, Robert
GEOLOGY QE 711.2	Ecology of fossils (1978)	McKerrow, W.S.
QL 737.C4 1982	Ecology of whales and dolphins	Gaskin, D. E.
HB171.5 .C2917 1987	Economic issues today	Carson, Robert Barry
JK 2160 .P47 1975	Electoral reform and voter participation	Phillips, Kevin P.
TA417.23.L67 1984	Electron beam analysis of materials	Loretto, M. H.
NE 642.B5	Engraved designs of William Blake (1967)	Binyon, Laurence
PN 3448.E6 1982	Epistolarity: approaches to a form	Altman, Janet Gurkin
PN 3495 .B5 1969	Epistolary novel in the late 18th century	Black, Frank Gees
PS 3515 .U789 Z82 1995	Every tub must sit on its own bottom	Plant, Deborah G.
PR 4147 .F7 1947	Fearful symmetry: a study of William Blake	Frye, Northrop
PN1995.9W6 M55 1991	Feminism without women	Modleski, Tania

Call Number	Title	Author
OVERSIZE LB1537 .F54 1982	Fifty-two preschool activity patterns	
E467 .A5 1968	Fighting Confederates	Anders, Curtis
TR850 .P54 1984	Filmmaker's handbook	Pincus, Edward
PN1995.9 W6 F55 1986	Films for women	Brunsdon, Charlotte
PR 873 .M5	Form of Victorian fiction	Miller, J. Hillis
FINE ARTS M1001 .M46 op.90 19--?	Fourth symphony	Mendelssohn-Bartholdy, Felix
PS3537.A426 F7 1961	Franny and Zooey	Salinger, J.D.
BF723.F68 C67 1985	Friendship and peer culture in the early years	Corsaro, William A.
E184.E2 F765 1982	From India to America	Chandrasekhar, S.
Q295 .E33 1987	Fuller explanation	Edmondson, Amy C.
QA76.758 .G47 1991	Fundamentals of software engineering	Ghezzi, Carlo
BF637.N4 F57 1981	Getting to yes	Fisher, Roger
ML410.P89 D7 1906	Giacomo Puccini	Dry, Wakeling
DD 247 .G6 H413 1983	Goebbels	Heiber, Helmut
DD 254 .S5 1943	Goebbels experiment	Sington, Derrick
PR9199.3 .A8 G66 1992	Good bones	Atwood, Margaret Eleanor
HQ 148.G66 1987b	Good girls, bad girls: sex trade workers and feminists face to face	Bell, Laurie
PA 3621.H6 1948	Greek literature in translation	Howe, George
BQ 4190 .P483	Handbook for Mankind	Thepwisutthimethi, Phra
GEOLOGY QE 718.K8	Handbook of paleontological techniques (1965)	Kummel, Bernhard
QA76 .H279 1990	Handbook of theoretical computer science	Leeuwen, Jan van
ND 237 .H667 1990	Hans Hofmann	Goodman, Cynthia
RA 781.7 .L8 1977	Hatha yoga for total health	Luby, Sue
F1776 .F57 1962	History of Cuba and its relations with the United States	Foner, Philip Sheldon
F592 .L57 1903	History of the expedition of Captain Lewis and Clark	Lewis, Meriwether
T 1940 .S46	History of the initiative in North Dakota	Selke, Albert George
B 132.Y6	History of Yoga (1982)	Worthington, Vivian
PN 1998 .A3 H553	Hitchcock--the murderous gaze	Rothman, William
OVERSIZE ND553.D24 R48 1966	Honore Daumier	Daumier, Honore Victorin
PS3563.O47 H6 1968	House made of dawn	Momaday, N. Scott
HQ784.T4 H68 1979	How to raise children in a TV world	Howe, Leland W.
PN 81 .H96 1994	Hyper/text/theory	Landow, George P.

Call Number	Title	Author
NE 642 .B5 1974	Illuminated Blake (1974)	Blake, William
LB 1060 .H63 1996	Implementing multiple intelligences: the New City School	Hoerr, Thomas R.
PS374 .W6 G55 1986	Indestructible woman in Faulkner, Hemingway, and Steinbeck	Gladstein, Mimi Reisel
E93 .I466 1986	Indian self-rule	Philp, Kenneth R.
Z 7128 .Y64 1981	International yoga bibliography	Jarrell, Howard R.
P121 .F75 1974	Introduction to language	Fromkin, Victoria
QA76.73 .P2 S36 1978	Introduction to programming and problem solving with PASCAL	Schneider, G. Michael
PN6112 .C33 1975	Introduction to theatre & drama	Cassady, Marshall
QA433 .D38 1979	Introduction to vector analysis	Davis, Harry F.
NK3880 .F43 1973	Islamic pottery	Fehrvare, Gza
TS156 .R25 1994	ISO 9000 book	Rabbit, John T.
OVERSIZE TX723 .I92 1991	Italy, a culinary journey	Luciano, Antony
OVERSIZE TX723 .D427 1989	Italy, the beautiful cookbook	De' Medici Stucchi, Lorenza
ND 1839 .L36 B76 1974	Jacob Lawrence	Lawrence, Jacob
PS3552 .A45 Z72 1986	James Baldwin	Bloom, Harold
ND 813 .M5	Joan Miro (1948	Greenberg, Clement
BL2015 .K3 C46 1986	Karma and creativity	Chapple, Christopher
Geology TN 805 .A4 K4 1993	Keystone coal industry manual	
QL737 .C432 F67 1994	Killer Whales	Ford, John K. B.
F636 .L56 1991	Land in her own name	Lindgren, H. Elaine
PG 3476 .P27 P613 1959	Last summer by Pasternak	Pasternak, Boris Leonidovich
LB 1032... 1987	Learning together and alone	Johnson, David W.
E467.1 .L4 N66 1991	Lee considered	Nolan, Alan T.
PS3562 .E42 L4 1979	Left hand of darkness	Le Guin, Ursula K.
PR 120 .G39 1990	Lesbian and gay writing...	Lilly, Mark
E185 .F8265 1990	Liberating visions	Franklin, Robert Michael
CB428 .M356 1989	Lipstick traces	Marcus, Greil
HQ784 .T4 P35 1986	Lively audience	Palmer, Patricia
BL1175 .G62 A3 1993	Living with Kundalini	Shepard, Leslie
F1435 .C82 1974	Lost civilization	Culbert, T. Patrick
PR 469 .W65 1983	Love and the woman question in Victorial literature	Blake, Kathleen
JK 1764 .M47 1984	Making something of ourselves	Merelman, Richard M.
BP223 .Z8 L5734 1992	Malcolm X	Gallen, David
E185.61 .L58 1989	Malcolm X speaks	X, Malcolm

Call Number	Title	Author
PQ 2344 Z5 F48 1986	Mallarme, Manet, and Redon	Florence, Penny
OVERSIZE ND553.M3 1992c	Manet	Stevenson, Lesley
E467.1.L4 C67 1977	Marble man	Connelly, Thomas Lawrence
N6853.D8 H6 1964	Marcel Duchamp: ready-mades	Hopps, Walter
HV5822.M3 G75 1977	Marihuana reconsidered	Grinspoon, Lester
PR 469 M35 M3	Marriage, duty and desire in Victorian poetry and drama	McGhee, Richard D.
E185.97.K5 C66 1991	Martin & Malcolm & America	Cone, James H.
HN59 .F66 1976	Mass advertising as social forecast	Gowles, Jib
BV 656.3 H66 1988	Mass media religion	Hoover, Stewart M.
HN57 .R79 1993	Master trend	Russell, Cheryl
TR 849 .A1 S33 1984	Masters of light	Schaefer, Dennis
Q370 .m38 1978	Maximum entropy formalism	Levine, Raphael D., et al
F1435 .C72 1984	Maya	Coe, Michael D.
NC257.B8 H57 1988	Michelangelo and his drawings	Hirst, Michael
E181 .A21 1911	Military studies	
DS 721 .S365 1974	Mind of China	Scharfstein, Ben-Ami
Geology QE 351 .M55 1992	Minerals and reactions at the atomic scale: transmission electron microscopy	Buseck, Peter R.
LB775.M8 F6 1966x	Montessori manual for teachers and parents	Fisher, Dorothea Frances
ML247.8.T47 K43 1985	Music in Terezin 1941-1945	Karas, Joza
PG 3476 .P27...1976	My sister, life and other poems...Boris Pasternak	Pasternak, Boris Leonidovich
D810 .P7 G317 1974	Mythical world of Nazi war propaganda	Baird, Jay W.
PN 1995 .B6173 1985	Narration in the fiction film	Bordwell, David
E98.T77 D44 1984	Nations within	Deloria, Vine
PS153.I52 L6 1983	Native American renaissance	Lincoln, Kenneth
E93 .N33 1992	Native Americans and public policy	Lyden, Fremont J., et al
PN1993.5.G3 L3813 1975ax	Nazi cinema	Leiser, Erwin
Geology QE 535.2.U6 P46 1976	New Madrid earthquakes of 1811-1812	Penick, James L.
N6535.N5 N38	New York Dada:Duchamp, Man Ray, Picabia	Duchamp, Marcel, et al
Geology QE 77 .C46 v.5	Northeastern section of the Geological Society of America	Roy, David C.
PG 3325.P73 1967	Notebooks for Crime and punishment	Dostoyevsky, Fyodor
GN2 .A27 v.30 pt.6 1929	Notes on Hopi clans	Lowie, Robert Harry
E241.B9 F58 1960	Now we are enemies	Fleming, Thomas J.

PZ1 .O11 1924	O. Henry memorial award prize stories	Williams, Blanche Colton, et al
BF 698 .L676	Objective approaches to personality assessment (1958)	Bass, Bernard M., et al
BF 698.4 .O23	Objective personality assessment: changing perspectives (1972)	Butcher, James Neal
ND 553 .R35 H6 1977b	Odilon Redon	Hobbs, Richard
ND 553 .R35 N4 1961	Odilon Redon	Moreau, Gustave, et al
ND 553 .R35 B43	Odilon Redon: fantasy and colour	Berger, Klaus
Nc 248 .R34 A4 1987	Odilon Redon: pastels	Bacou, Roseline
PN 56 .T37...1995	Of two minds: hypertext pedagogy and poetics	Joyce, Michael
F592.7 .C543 1979	Only one man died	Chuinard, Eldon G.
Q175 .P8822 1984b	Order out of chaos	Prigogine, I.
PG 3456 .A1 1965	Oxford Chekhov	Chekhov, Anton Pavlovich
Geology TN 805.A5 P35 1986	Paleoenvironmental and tectonic controls in coal-forming basins of the U.S.	Lyons, Paul C., et al
GEOLOGY QE 720	Paleoocology, concepts and application (1981)	Dodd, J Robert
GEOLOGY QE 718	Paleotechniques (1989)	Feldmann, Rodney M., et al
AS 36 .F5x	Paradox of privacy (1984)	Gillis, Christina Marsden
Jf 493 .U6 Z56 1986	Participatory democracy:populism revived	Zimmerman, Joseph Francis
LB1140.35 .G74 S64 1993	Peaceful classroom	Smith, Charles A.
TS 755 .P3 T33 1985	Pearls: their origin, treatment and identification	Taburiaux, Jean
HQ734 .S266 1972	Peoplemaking	Satir, Virginia M.
OVERSIZE NK1710 .C6 1949	Period furnishings	Clifford, Chandler Robbins
F 3101 .E33 A3413 1977b	Persona non grata : an envoy in Castro's Cuba	Edwards, Jorge
NX 454 .H36 1981	Phantoms of the imagination: fantasy in art and literature from Blake to Dali	Hammacher, Abraham Marie
TR145 .M57 1984	Photographic science	Mitchell, Earl N.
PG 3456 .P43 M3	Platonov: a play in four acts and five scenes	Chekhov, Anton Pavlovich
PR 5550 1909	Poems of Alfred Tennyson	Tennyson, Alfred, Baron
PR 5550 .E98 1898	Poetic and dramatic works of Alfred, lord Tennyson	Tennyson, Alfred, Baron
N 7483 .G73...1985	Political origins of abstract-expressionist art criticism	Herbert, James D.
B 132 .Y6	Popular yoga(1972)	Kuvalayananda, Swami

Call Number	Title	Author
HM 133 .V67	Positive Peer Culture	Vorrath, Harry H.
PN 1998.2 .V66 1991	Postmodern auteurs	Von gunden, Kenneth
N6494.P66 P67 1990	Postmodern perspectives	Risatti, Howard
Geology QH 212.S3 C64 1975	Practical Scanning electron microscopy: electron and ion microprobe analaysis	Goldstein, Joseph
LB1140.35.C74 C66 1987	Pre-school play activities	Conner, Edwina
E51 .H337 v.54 1965	Prehistoric Maya settlements in the Belize Valley	Willey, Gordon Randolph
GEOLOGY QE711.2	Principles of paleontology (1978)	Raup, David M.
JC 423 .O75 1985	Problem of participation	Osbun, Lee Ann
QA76.9A43 A34a 1990	Proceedings of the ... annual ACM-SIAM Symposium on Discrete Algorithms	
HM 261 .S6 1939	Public opinion in a democracy	Smith, Charles william
HQ 76.8 .U5 ...1993	Queer in America: sex, the media, and the closets of power	Signorile, Michelangelo
PR 3664.C43 E2 1982	Rape of Clarissa	Eagleton, Terence
TA 781 .K85 1978	Rating the exercises	Kuntzleman, Charles T.
PR 3664.C43 1979	Reading Clarissa: the struggles of interpretation	Warner, William Beatty
HD1387 .R357 1977	Readings in real property valuation principles	American Institute of Real Estate Appraisers
HD1387 .B69 1975	Real estate appraisal terminology	Boyce, Byrl N.
HD 1375.R43 1985	Real Estate Sales Handbook	Realtors National Marketing Institute
PS3513.I74 R4 1963	Reality sandwiches	Ginsberg, Allen
HV 1431.B7 1990	Reclaiming youth at risk: our hope for the future	Brendtro, Larry K.
DS 748 .S7453	Records of the grand historian of China	Ssu-ma, Ch'ien
TA683.2 .F4 1973	Reinforced concrete fundamentals	Ferguson, Phil Moss
F1435.3.R3 K35 1981	Religion of the Maya	Kampen, M. E.
JC 423 .G74 1985	Retrieving democracy: in search of civic equality	Green, Philip
PS 3553.U73...1981	Revolt of the perverts	Curzon, Daniel
Geology QE 397 .D44 1962	Rock-forming minerals	Deer, W. A.
H1 .A4 v.427 1976	Role of the mass media in American politics	Martin, L. John
PR 590 .R59 1993	Romantic poetry	Kroeber, Karl, et al
PG 3476 .P27...1958	Safe conduct: an autobiogrpahy...Boris Pasternak	Pasternak, Boris Leonidovich
BF 1576 1992	Salem witch crisis	Gragg, Larry Dale

Call Number	Title	Author
BR563.N4 H867 1981	Sanctified Church (Zora Neale Hurston	Hurston, Zora Neale
QB401 .S38 1986	Satellites	Burns, Joseph A., et al
Geology QE 471.2 .S25	Scanning electron microscopy in the study of sediments	Whalley, W. Brian
PN 162 .S45 1986	Scholarly editing in the computer age	Shillingsburg, Peter L.
QP360 .S63 1983	Science and moral priority	Sperry, Roger Wolcott
B 132 .Y6	Science of Yoga(1979)	Taimni, I. K.
LB775 .M785 1966	Secret of childhood	Montessori, Maria
LB 1060.L392 1991	Seven ways of knowing: teaching for multiple intelligences	Lazear, David G.
E185.97.D73 A26 1971	Seventh son	Du Bois, W. E. B.
PR 3664.C43...1984	Sex and enlightenment; women in Richardson and Diderot	Goldberg, Rita
RJ507.S49 S49 1990	Sexually abused male	Hunter, Mic
D 582.G7	Ship that Changed the World (1985)	Van der Vat, Dan
LB1532 .P47 1989	Small wonders	Perdue, Peggy K.
HV 95 .D56 1991	Social welfare: politics and public policy	DiNitto, Diana M.
DK266 .M354 1993	Soviet Union	McCauley, Martin
DP 203 C3 1982	Spain, 1808-1975	Carr, Raymand
DP 66 .S55 1965	Spain: a modern history	Smith, Rhea Marsh
GV 716.M 85 1993	Sport marketing	Mullin, Bernard James
GV 176 .S32 1995	Sports marketing: it's not just a game anymore	Schaaf, Phil
DS 734.9 S8W3	Ssu-ma Ch*ien, grand historian of China	Watson, Burton
Energy TP 325 .S713 1982	Stach's Textbook of Coal Petrology	Stach, Erich
Z 104 .K9...1976	Statistical methods in cryptanalysis	Kullback, Solomon
KF4119 .S73 1980	Statutory mandates and agency enforcement	Council of School Attorneys
HE 8689.8 .S73 1990	Stay tuned: a concise history of American broadcasting	Sterling, Christopher H.
TA684 .S24 1971	Steel structures	Salmon, Charles G.
GEOLOGY QE 720	Structure and classification of paleocommunities (1976)	Scott, Robert W., et al
PS153.I52 S8 1983	Studies in American Indian literature	Allen, Paula Gunn
PL 2253 .S8	Studies in Chinese literary genres	Birch, Cyril
E 181.A21 1911	Studies military and diplomatic, 1775-1865	Adams, Charles Francis
PE 1559 .D47 1969	Study of metre	Omond, Thomas Stewart
N6465.S9 D35	Symbolists and symbolism	Delevoy, Robert L.
P120.S48 C73 1995	Talking difference	Crawford, Mary
GV1007 .B28 1982	Teaching badminton	Ballou, Palph B.

141

Books Lost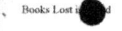

Call Number	Title	Author
GV836.35 .T48 1989	Teaching swimming	Thomas, David G.
HQ784.T4 L34 1981	Television's impact on children and adolescents	Singer, Jerome L.
HQ784.T4 S56 1981	Television, imagination, and aggression	Lake, Sara
940.5318 A141c	The children we remember	Abells, Chana Byers
973.7 L657f 1968	The first book of the Civil War	Levenson, Dorothy
E 757.A37 1985	Theodore Roosevelt: an autobiography	Roosevelt, Theodore
P90 .L48 1991	Theories of human communication	Littlejohn, Stephen W.
DP 43 .O53 1954	This is Spain	Olague, Ignacio
F592.7 .W46 1926	Trail of Lewis and Clark	Wheeler, Olin Dunbar
F592.7 .S124 1950ax	Two captains west	Salisbury, Albert P.
HF 5681 .B2...1990	Understanding financial statements	Gill, James O.
PR 468 .S6 R4 1975	Victorian conventions	Reed, John Robert
DA 533 .Q5 1941a	Victorian prelude, a history of English manners	Quinlan, Maurice James
PR 468 .S6 V5 1978	Victorians	Lerner, Laurence
PN1995.9 W6M84 1989	Visual and other pleasures	Mulvey, Laura
PS 3204 .S81934	Walt Whitman: representative selections	Whitman, Walt
HC110.P6 G36 1995	War against the poor	Gans, Herbert J.
D810.P7 G338 1978	War that Hitler won	Herzstein, Robert Edwin
D805.C9 J413 1995	We are children just the same	Krizkoya, Marie Ruth
TX723.2.S65 B37 1990	We called it macaroni	Barr, Nancy Verde
E185 .S87 1970	What country have I?	Storing, Herbert J.
NE 642.B5 1978	William Blake	Paley, Morton D.
NE 642.B5	William Blake: book illustrator: 1972	Easson, Roger R.
NE 642.B5 1975	William Blake: selected engravings	Blake, William
PN 4874 .H4 A3	William Randolph Hearst: a portain in his own words	Hearst, William Randolph
Dewey F F G742wa	Wind in the Willows	Grahame, Kenneth
PS153.I52 C57 1990	Winged words	Coltelli, Laura
BQ1138 .W58 1987	Wisdom of Buddhism	Humphreys, Christmas
OVERSIZE NK1149.5 .C34 1979	Women artists of the arts and crafts movement	Callen, Anthea
PN1995.9W6 B4 1974	Women in focus	Betancourt, Jeanne
PS 153.N5 W33 1995	Women of the Harlem renaissance	Perry, Ruth
PR 858.E65...1980	Women, letters, and the novel	Wall, Cheryl A.
QP411 .E28 1984	Wonder of being human	Eccles, John C.
PE 1559.H3 1976	Words into rhythm	Harding, Denys Clement Wyatt
LA 222 .W67 1994	World Class schools: an evolving concept	Jenkins, John M., et al

N 6853 .D8 T6 1966	World of Marcel Duchamp	Tomkins, Calvin
QL737.C22 G625 1995	World of the coyote	Grady, Wayne
Geology QD 945 .N83 1966	X-ray diffraction methods	Nuffield, E. W.
LB1140.4 .C644 1986	Year 'round activities for four-year-old children	Coletta, Anthony J.
B 132 .Y6	Yoga and beyond(1972)	Feuerstein, Georg
B 132.Y6	Yoga as philosophy and religion (1973)	Dasgupta, Surendra Nath
B 132 .Y6	Yoga Dictionary(1956)	Wood, Ernest
HF 5415 .B38 1976	Your career in marketing	Beaumont, John Appleton
RJ496.A86 I54 1988	Your hyperactive child	Ingersoll, Barbara D.
BQ9299.H854 L6375 1993	Zen doctrine of no-mind	Suzuki, Daisetz Teitaro
PQ9265.4 .O36 1959	Zen for the West	Ogata, Sohaku
D 604 .R62 1994	Zeppelin in combat	Brooks, Peter W.
TL 657 .B76 1992b	Zeppelin: rigid airships	Robinson, Douglas Hill
D 604 .C76 1993	Zeppelins of World War I	Cross, Wilbur
PS 3515. U789 1991	Zora	Nathiri, N. Y.
PS 3515 .U789 Z96 1986	Zora Neale Hurston	Bloom, Harold

143

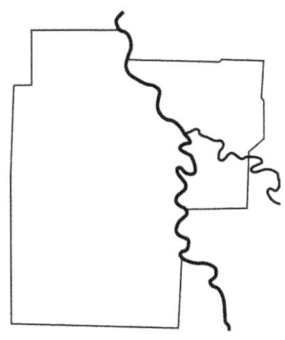

Behind the Scenes at the University

Kendall Baker, Bruce Gjovig, Randy Newman

From *Behind the Scenes* (2002)

CLOSING THE UNIVERSITY

I've said many times that the decision to close the University was the toughest decision I've ever made in my academic career. Friday night I was out on the Smith Hall dike working with the students to try to get that one up high enough so that we could try to save the area, and my cell phone rang. They said it looks like the Water Plant is going down, you've got to come down here, we're going to have to talk about what we have to do. I went down to Plant Services and walked in the door and they said the city has closed the Water Plant down, it's flooded and there is nothing that they can do.

At first I didn't want to accept the consequences of that. The three vice presidents were there and we began to talk about it and I was thinking, what can we do? They are telling us that we've got ten million gallons of water which will, if we ration it, last us for a week and so we started talking about what our options were. At first I did not want to accept the magnitude of what had happened. We sat there and talked for an hour and a half or more and finally it became clear. I can remember very clearly then saying, "Okay, we have to close." The reaction from the people that I was talking to was, we don't have any choice. We are not going to be able to maintain sanitary conditions, we are not going to be able to feed anyone, we are not going to be able to operate any of our laboratories, we are not going to be able to do any of the things that an educational institution does.

I didn't want to believe it, but it finally became very clear that we just didn't have any choice. I left Plant Services that night and went home with the greatest sense of resignation. I was as depressed and disturbed at that point as I was at any point in the entire set of events and circumstances. I didn't want to do it. I just didn't want to believe that I had to do it. It became absolutely clear the more that we talked about it and the more that we looked at the parameters that there is just no way. We just couldn't do it, we couldn't keep the University open.

Kendall Baker
President, University of North Dakota

WHAT TO SAVE, WHAT TO LET GO

There were some very tough decisions about what to try to save and what to let go. The library was easy and number one. We all knew immediately that we had to try to do something about the Law Library and the Chester Fritz. All of the indicators were that the water was going to come right in both of those areas and we felt that was going to happen up until literally the very last minute. We knew we had to go after the library right away.

The Computer Center is another wonderful example. We didn't actually even remember it until Sunday afternoon. All of a sudden we realized my gosh, what are we going to do? If we lose the Computer Center then the whole North Dakota University System is down. Nobody is going to get paid, we can't track anything and that's when we had this incredible situation with John the truck driver. He had been there earlier on Sunday with his rig and this Allied Van Lines truck parked right out in front of Plant Services and he'd been over helping us move things. As he was leaving that afternoon he said, "If you need anything else, here's my cell phone number and here's my business number." I wrote these things down. We all were carrying around these pieces of paper with all these things written down. It was just amazing.

When we realized the Computer Center was at risk, which happened at the five o'clock session on Sunday, I called John on his cell phone. The first time I couldn't get in, the second time I did. I said, "John, remember me? We need a truck because we've got to take our Computer Center down and we have to get it to Fargo." He said, "Fine, what time do you need me?" He came over with his rig and we went through and started pulling the wires out of the Computer Center and taking it down.

I remember the decision to let the Energy and Environmental Research Center (EERC) go as though it were yesterday. The call came through to LeRoy Sondreal, head of the University's physical infrastructure. We were there together and they told me what the circumstances were and I just simply said we can't do it, we have to pull the plug. We've got too much risk of life, too much risk of fire and all those kinds of things. We just can't do it. We have got to take it down. Those were exceedingly difficult decisions. I knew how much equipment was in the basement of the EERC but we couldn't run the risk anymore. Not too terribly long after we made that decision is when LeRoy went into the Nutrition Lab and found the fire about to start there. We made the right decision but let me tell you, it was not an easy one to make.

The way that we really identified the jewels of the University were through the knowledge and the expertise of the people that were here. We were in the very fortunate position of having people who have worked with the University for a long period of time and who, as a consequence, valued the traditions and valued its history and at the same time knew the things that we had to do in order to be able to preserve that. LeRoy said at one of our early nine o'clocks that we need to take the University down so that we could put it back up in a way that we would preserve the most. That was the philosophy. From day one. Take the University down in such a way that we can save as much as possible when we put it back up. We lost a lot in the process - the Medical School and EERC are prime examples, the basement of the Union. None of these were easy decisions.

Kendall Baker
President, University of North Dakota

THE KEYS TO THE KINGDOM

This is my sixth year as President of the University and until the flood I did not have the master keys of the University. I now do. There are about six of them and they are on a ring and the ring is actually soldered together. You know how a key ring normally has a place where you can take the keys off? Actually they were soldered on the key ring so that you can't get the keys off because these are the master keys to every nook and cranny in the University. They will open any door and get you anywhere in the University. Friday night or Saturday we made the decision that we would produce five sets of those because we had to have people who would have access to any part of the University. Then we set up a situation where we would always have one of the University officers literally on 24-hour duty and whoever was going to do that had to have the keys so that we could get into the places that we needed to get into. That's how I got my keys to the University. After the flood was over everybody was supposed to give their keys back but I said, "No way." Everybody else has given theirs up. I haven't given mine up. I've got my keys and I actually continue to use them.

Kendall Baker
President, University of North Dakota

REOPENING THE UNIVERSITY:
A SIGNAL TO THE COMMUNITY

When we opened the Summer School on May 8th, people thought I was nuts to do that. We had to do it in order to be able to convince our students, our faculty and our staff that we could come back. The longer we waited to start doing the things that we do as an institution, the longer we instill doubt, the longer that we make problems for ourselves. At least, that's what my thinking was. Our goal was to become functionally operational. Summer School was perhaps the best demonstration of our ability to be functionally operational. It was a statement, it was a signal to our students and to our community that we were coming back. It was also important to our faculty and staff. We needed to have some goals here. We've got to move forward, we have to be positive. We have to be thinking in terms of things that we're going to accomplish and setting some of these goals which seem tough. I think it gave some motivation as well.

People thought I was crazy. I can remember the looks on people's faces when I was asked. I said, yep, that's what we are gonna do, we are going to open. That's one of the few times that people have to accept the fact that you make a statement as a president and then they turn around when you leave and say, is he nuts? They didn't say it directly to me. No one said, you can't be serious. At least not that I heard. Of course people have teased me a lot about it now. It was a very deliberate and very serious decision because I think that we needed goals, we needed focus, we needed purpose, we needed motivation, we needed positive messages. Being functionally operational for Summer School was a very, very important component of recovery.

Kendall Baker
President, University of North Dakota

THE HUB OF THE COMMUNITY

I began to meet with some community officials and leaders who ended up out at the Rural Technology area at the University. That became the hub of the community. All of us were concerned about the community, the University, the citizens, our business community. We all felt, particularly the business community, that the faster we got people into their jobs that that would help with the recovery. We all turned our attention to getting those businesses up and running that could, and then the University came up with this plan to allow some of the University space to serve as a temporary home for those people who were displaced.

Randy Newman
President, First National Bank of Grand Forks

UNIVERSITY-BUSINESS RELATIONS

As a result of the flood, the University has a new respect for the business community, and sees itself being far more flexible and adaptable in serving the business community. The business community also has a new respect for the University, what we do out here in terms of the Center for Innovation, what the College of Business and other departments out here do. There's a tremendous amount of good will. Those 30-some companies that were on campus have a new love for the University that was never here before. Immediately after this the Chamber invited the Dean of the Business College and myself to sit on their board. I don't think that's an accident. I've headed a delegation to Washington to talk to SBA about responding to the business community. I don't think that was any accident. That's all, I think, in respect for what we did after the flood.

Bruce Gjovig
Director, Center for Innovation

THE FLOOD WAS A MOTIVATOR

In the University of the 21st Century, there will be much, much closer linkage between institutions and their communities. There will be closer relationships and partnerships between the University and public and private groups. There will be all sorts of technologically facilitated instruction and interaction. Because of the circumstances that the flood put us in, I felt that we had an opportunity to begin to develop the kind of prototype of the University of the 21st Century right here in Grand Forks.

First, we created the virtual University. What was the virtual University? The virtual University was the University of North Dakota operating basically in a technological environment. We didn't have any space, there wasn't any place we could go. We didn't have water, we had porta potties! We couldn't go to a laboratory, but we could find the place where we could put an awful lot of people with an awful lot of computing power. Our Telecom people came through unbelievably. They wired up that room over in the Rural Technology Center so that every one of our units could have technological capability. With that technological capability they were able to begin communicating with their students, with their faculty, with their staff, with professional organizations, with granting agencies. They weren't doing any of this out of their laboratories, they weren't doing any of it out of their classrooms, they weren't doing any of it out of their offices, because they didn't have any. They had a room. It was a big room, but we took a university with 5,000 full and part-time employees and more than 11,000 students, and put it in one room. We said the way that you function and operate is electronically.

Another good example of the University of the 21st Century is the way that we responded to businesses in our community. We had thirty-three businesses that worked at the University of North Dakota between the 1st of May and the 1st of August. We had judges using the courtroom over in the Law School and having their offices over there. We had a number of law offices that moved into the Law building. We had accounting businesses. We had David Badman, who is a fabulous jeweler and a wonderful artist, doing his work on campus.

EERC has been extensively involved in all the conversations about dikes and diversions and what will we do in the future. Our Sociology Department's been doing housing surveys. We've got faculty that are involved in the reimaging process downtown. You name it, the University people have been part of the community recovery process. A lot of what we did is moving in the direction in which the University is going to have to move in the 21st Century. I don't have any doubt that the flood has helped us a great deal in that regard. We're not there yet, nobody is there yet. But, by golly, we're moving towards it and making as much progress as anybody else. The flood was, without question, an important stimulus and important motivator. We were going that way, but when you have a disaster like we had there's a lot more reason to move that way and to move more quickly. And that's what we are doing.

Kendall Baker
President, University of North Dakota

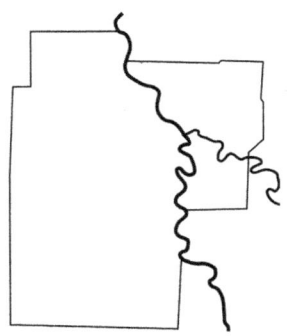

The Unfolding

Janet Rex

Water glistens in the grass. I stop us—Caitlin, five years old, and Max, our Golden Retriever, leashed for his bedtime walk. Max sniffs the water. Am I seeing correctly? On previous walks, we would see the river flowing past, carrying branches, held by the forearms and elbows of our sandbags, but now the stealth of the water is nearing Belmont Road, having risen beyond the sandbags on the embankment protecting the Myra Museum. I feel a sinking resignation as I turn us toward home.

Our pre-flood fight is receding into the darkness with the failing sandbag walls. Cliff, my husband, and I have taken shifts working within the relays of hands passing sandbags through the joyous sunny days full of hope and the silent serious nights when we were racing around the clock to build the walls high enough. Many of our neighbors could not believe that the flood would rise to the level of our ranch-style homes at the hundred-year flood level, saying, "If it gets to my house, it will flood all of Grand Forks." Unlike these skeptics, the flood warnings and the daily sounds of helicopter surveillance have created a constant state of panic in me, propelling me to trek up and down the stairs bringing boxes of Christmas ornaments, baby clothes, and stacks of books up to the main floor from the basement. I brought up as much as I could before that last afternoon when I lay feverish in the living room hemmed in by the piles in the house. Our toilets were burping and gurgling, and I was thankful that Cliff had plugged the basement drains.

Now, as we enter the house from our walk, I hear Cliff's anxious question, "Where did you go?" During this period, panicky feelings occur whenever one's family members are out of sight.
I tell Cliff, "The water has breached the sandbags and is almost to Belmont Road!" I call Malva Waters, and I tell her we are heading their way. Malva and Jack Waters have kindly invited us to join them if we need to escape a flooding house, and now we must flee the city before bedtime. Caitlin shows me she has packed her clothes in her blue doll suitcase. We pack our bags, pillows, Max, and Toby the scavenger fish into the car; and we head toward Jack and Malva Waters' place. Their orderly home is a relief for us and some other flood refugees. We are welcomed, and Toby is set free to swim in their aquarium. Max will sleep outside.

We set out the next day for my parents' farmhouse in Wisconsin. As we drive down I-29 toward Fargo, the scene is unbelievable. What is normally a freeway in the middle of flat farmland has become an isthmus between seas. The fields are inundated by melted water from the ice storm and the eight winter blizzards.

The terror recedes as we leave the Red River valley, yet the calm of the Wisconsin farmyard seems so unreal in comparison. At the farm, my dad, my mom, and warm meals welcome us. Sunlight stretches protectively across us on their enclosed front porch. For the foreseeable future, we must leave Max trapped in this small front porch to avoid Woofy their colorful protective mutt.

Next, we visit my sister, Barb, and her husband, Jim, in Madison, Wisconsin. While we are there, Grand Forks makes the national news. The television shows an underwater, downtown Grand Forks engulfed in flames. I gasp, because this seems so unbelievable! We stare at one another and wonder when we will be able to return.

We certainly will have extra time to visit Cliff's family. On the internet, Cliff notices cheap airline tickets to the East Coast, so we make a trip to see his parents in New Jersey. We enjoy New York pizza, and we wait like driftwood on the beach collecting seashells. Cliff monitors his dad's computer for updates. Finally, weeks after we have left Grand Forks, we find out that the water is receding, and the city is allowing people back into their homes. We fly back to Wisconsin, pick up our car, leave Caitlin with my parents, and drive back to face the disaster of our home.

The city of Grand Forks is still a ghost town. Our sunlit home appears normal and welcoming as we enter the driveway; but within our home, we see that the framed "Oriental Poppies" poster by Georgia O'Keeffe has wrinkled under the glass from the dampness. We peer down into the basement, and we see a rim of wet against the wall. My two commemorative framed UND plaques are floating on top of the water. We are without electricity, telephone, and heat.

We get a hotel room in Fargo, and we drive back and forth each day to work on the house. We must hire someone to pump the water from the basement before we can clean the place and find people to replace our services. Before we depart for our first morning of work, I feel so overwhelmed that I sit and cry in the Fargo hotel lobby. Each night, I swim to relax in the colorfully lit pool, for each day we must face the real water.

First, we work with someone to pump the water down the driveway to the storm sewer. After the pumping, we descend into the darkness, wading through in rubber boots. We face the mounds of our wet things—our entertainment center and southwestern blue couch, our crib, books, chairs, carpet, washer, dryer, many other miscellaneous things, soggy walls, and our fridge full of a thawed turkey and rotting food.

Our insurance agent surveys the state of the wreckage. We are luckier than some people, because we heeded the warnings, and we took out flood insurance that went into force just days before the flooding. Still the insurance agent, standing in the mucky mess, says, "You two will take a bath." Most of our possessions, such as our refrigerator, are not covered by the flood insurance. A freezer would have been covered. The washer and dryer reclaim little of their worth. Although the damage is extensive, the insurance agent is able to send in a claim for $10,000.

Later in the summer, I sign up for $1,000 from the "Angel" fund, a generous donation by an anonymous benefactor. We later learn the donor is Joan Kroc, the billionaire widow of Ray Kroc, the McDonald's Corporation founder. She donates $15 million for distribution in $2,000 increments to each family affected by the flooding. As the funding dwindles, city officials decrease the allotted amount; and after I wait in a long line to sign up for the "Angel" fund, we receive a check for $1,000. The "Angel" fund and the insurance settlement help us somewhat with the financial loss.

After the insurance analysis, we remove a screen from one of the basement windows. Cliff flings Star Trek books and other items out onto the lawn, and I pick them up and move them onto the berm. Cliff cuts the carpeting and saws the southwestern couch into pieces. The carpeting, in buckets, our fridge, and other large items must be carried, dripping wet, up the stairs and out through the front door. Although we put down a plastic runner, the main floor carpeting from the basement to the front door is ruined in the process. The berm pile grows high with our things. When we drive around, we see a house sitting on a car. We see graffiti on homes, such as "Home Sweet Home" or "49 Feet, My Ass!" And everywhere we see huge piles of belongings. Our cars, like the cars of our neighbors, get flat tires from driving around town, because there are nails scattered throughout the streets.

During this initial cleanup phase, many businesses are closed, but the empty Kmart parking lot hosts donated pallets of bottled water and bleach. Red Cross and Salvation Army food trucks ring bells as they drive through the streets or park in the Walmart parking lot to give out warm meals. Initially we take some meals, but later Cliff accurately states, "We don't need to take this charity any longer. We can leave it for others."

In the midst of our flood cleanup, Cliff returns to teaching at UND. We pick Caitlin up in Wisconsin. We get a room in the UND dorms, and Caitlin will go part time to the University Children's Center. As we enter the dormitory, there are piles of donated clothing near the doorway, and I pick out a white terry cloth bathrobe, decorated by a gold thread moon and stars.

Caitlin is so happy to be in the dorms. Since she is an only child, we must always seek out other children for her to play with. Now there are other children everywhere. She is invited for cake at a birthday party. She makes a new friend. She is so happy about the flood that she says, "I hope this happens again!"

One day, I look out the dorm window, and I remember a puzzling pre-flood dream. The dream opens with an image similar to the Chevrolet logo, but lacking the diagonal lines. This image of a horizontal, rectangular cross, with short central arms, precedes a scene in which two people, Ann Sande and Karen Katrinak from our church, are busy moving around. I ask my dream, "What are they doing?" The dream responds with a white lotus flower unfolding and a voice stating, "It's in the unfolding." Now I see that the dorm is that same rectangular cross-like shape as in my dream. I have just read a newspaper article telling how Ann is working with the City Council on flood concerns, and I have just heard how Karen is dealing with her own flood issues. I remember my dream, and it seems surreal that all of these elements coalesce at the same time.

We finish flood cleanup. Cliff power washes the basement, and I hand wash the remaining muck with additional bleach. After the services are back in place, we can return to living in our home, although we must live amidst the mounds of our things on our main floor while the basement dries out over the summer. We move some of the mounds into the garage.

At this point, I've been involved with Habitat for Humanity since 1995, performing tasks such as getting lamp donations and helping to select families. Now Habitat calls on me to give more. Since I'm currently a stay-at-home mom, someone from Habitat suggests, "You're not working. You could coordinate a Habitat Home." I take it on, and I spend my summer, sometimes from 6 a.m. to 10 p.m., seeking and coordinating donations for food and drinks, as well as volunteers, lumber, heating experts, electricians, and plumbers. Many people come into Grand Forks from out of town to volunteer. I recruit some of them for the Habitat Home. Caitlin spends some of her time with me at the Habitat Home hanging out with the neighboring family, a previous Habitat family, eager to put in their sweat equity by babysitting for her. At one point, early in the construction, rainwater fills the newly dug hole of the Habitat Home; and I frantically pump out the water. I am thankful that Jack Reese, from the Rose Flower Shop, can provide the construction coordination, telling the volunteers how to build the home. I am thankful for the help from the volunteers, the Habitat families, the members of the Habitat Board of Directors, and Eliot Glassheim, President of the Board of Directors, as well as Founder, of the Red River Valley Habitat for Humanity.

Other tasks over the next year come to me through Cliff. The Natural Hazards Center in Boulder, Colorado is looking for someone to give them reports about the flood repair, and I agree to help them. I interview city officials and find data and information for them from news reports. Since our U.S. disaster analysis is concurrent with work in Canada, we must await the signature of the Queen of England before we can begin our project. As a second project, I receive articles about the flood, and I write abstract summaries of these articles. Thirdly, Cliff, Kathleen Tiemann, and I, among other people, help Alice Fothergill from the Natural Hazards Center get her research project off the ground, which leads to her publication of *Heads Above Water: Gender, Class, and Family in the Grand Forks Flood*, SUNY, 2004.

We bring our dog, Max, back from Wisconsin. Then one day I arrive home late from the Habitat Home, and Caitlin runs out to the car, saying, "Look what we have!" She takes me to the back porch to meet Shiloh, a soft Golden Retriever puppy of frenetic excitement, jumping, leaping, licking, and smelling of puppy breath. Cliff and Caitlin have acquired Shiloh for our new beginning. I wish I could feel more excited, but I fear that much of the dog care will fall to me.

We also find that this small gold puppy plays, nips, and torments our older dog, Max, now developing rapidly growing tumors. By November, a tumor has grown quickly in his mouth, displacing his teeth, and he cannot eat without his mouth bleeding. The vets can do nothing for him, and we must put him to sleep. Cliff, Caitlin, and I take him to the vet. Cliff sits with him until the end. Toby, also, has not survived his aquarium home. He disappeared, eaten one day by another fish in Jack and Malva Waters' aquarium.

Normally, I would attend calming meditation with Tamar Read. She has provided funding to build the Lotus Meditation Center. Throughout the Lotus construction period prior to the flood, we would sit amidst the sawdust for meditation. We would talk about the *Jataka Tales* or the teachings of Jack Kornfield. Although I am too busy to attend her Fall building dedication, we will now have a new beautiful meditation center with gold oak benches, trim, and flooring edged by red carpeting. Gold sconce lamps tip the light upwards. Large rectangular windows allow plenty of light, and a round window looks out upon the treetops. It is a glorious new beginning—a glorious unfolding!

We faced a lot of work and a lot of stress. We did what had to be done. We cleaned. We repaired. We helped others. Yet, as I summarized the flood articles, one article stood out from the others. It reports that families who lose nothing or those who lose everything fare better than those who lose basements. For those who lose basements will face higher rates of divorce, and within a few years, it will become true for Cliff and me.

Yet, the flood also brought people together. The Summer Performing Arts organized the play, "Keep the Faith," a glorious performance of renewal, reminding us of the times we would cluster with our neighbors in the streets outside of our homes sharing sorrows and assistance. We helped one another to find service experts, rebuild, dedicate a new meditation center, build one family a new Habitat Home, and create our new community.

It Was Like Nothing Else in My Life Up to Now

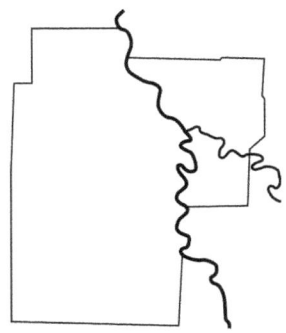

Josh Roiland

On a still summer night in the last year of last century an overweight woman in a wheelchair appeared, as if an apparition, under a street lamp in a parking lot on the west end of campus. I had not seen her when I pulled my car in. It was an hour till midnight, and I was covered in sand.

I'd spent the night playing volleyball and had returned home to married student housing where I was summering with a friend's wife, while he interned in Minneapolis. She was a nurse who worked nights, and I was an English major lazing between my junior and senior year. We rarely saw each other; the only complication in our cohabitation resulted from my inability to lift the toilet seat when I got up to pee in the middle of the night. In the mornings we'd cross paths and she'd tell me, again, that it was no fun to come home and sit in piss.

That night in the dark parking lot, the woman rolled her heavy body from behind a street-lamp. "Excuse me," she said, coming closer.

"Hi!" she said cheerfully. "Can you, uh—would you be able to give me a ride home?"

She worked at a telemarketing place near the corner of University Ave. and 42nd St. Work had let out, but the buses had stopped running, and she needed a way home. She crossed the busy intersection and wheeled into the expansive parking lot waiting for someone to help her. I was tired and dirty. I just wanted to slink into the stuffy efficiency, shower, and distract myself to sleep with PlayStation. But here she sat.

"Sure," I said. "Sure, I'll give you a ride home."

I knew before I got in the car. I had known for weeks even though no one would tell me. The phone calls changed. My mom barely spoke, her voice vacant. My dad tried to distract me with sports talk and questions about classes, but he was distracted himself. I knew. I knew it had come back.

Every minute of that five-hour drive home from Duluth, where I was a freshman finance major, brought me closer to realizing what I knew. It was Thanksgiving break. My friend Jordan drove us both home. I told him, "There's something going on with my mom." We talked about anything else until that last mile of gravel before my house. We passed over a short rise and between the barren tree line where I had shot my first deer. Corn stubble stretched from both sides of the road. Then, confirmation: my dad's pickup truck parked on the road, waiting to intercept us. A quarter mile away, our small house with the large picture window loomed.

My dad gave Jordan twenty bucks for gas as I got out of the car and threw my stuff in the back. We took off around the section, same as we always did, road hunting for pheasants or scouting deer. But it was not the same. I knew it was coming. In the stillness, I braced myself.

"Your mother is sick," he said, his first words as we began down the road. *Sick*, a euphemism we would wear out in the years ahead. "She has six lesions on her spine." I remember how odd that word sounded. What did he mean *lesions*?

"Tumors," he said. "She has six tumors on her spine."

I felt like a stranger sitting there. What was this new language? I didn't know how to speak. I didn't cry. We turned left onto the second mile. Finally, I asked about her prognosis. He didn't know.

"She could live five years or five months or five days," he said. The road ahead looked the same, but felt somehow worse. Then another left, and we passed my mom's parents' house on mile three.

"How are they doing?" I asked.

"Not good," he said.

On that last mile, before we crossed the threshold of our driveway—that slow curve bending toward the small house where my mom and her mom sat waiting—I told him I was transferring to UND. None of us could have imagined the flood that was to come.

I moved to Grand Forks four months after the mandatory evacuations. Summer was starting to recede and campus bloomed with new and returning students. I saw no scars. But then, how could I? I experienced the flood from the periphery, only feeling it obliquely from friends' letters and emails. I read spent stories of sandbagging around Smith Hall—my dorm that fall—then dikes breaking, then exodus, fire. In person, I couldn't reconcile that damage with the patina of hope that a new school and a new school year brought. I hadn't been there and I couldn't see the rot extant throughout the city.

But I tried.

In those first weeks, my roommate and I would funnel our way downtown. We stopped at the Sorlie Bridge and tried to imagine the waterline on the trusses. Then we headed down Belmont and over to Lincoln Drive where we drove slow through the ghost town. Houses ruined inside and out as the water spread, then stayed, before finally ebbing back below flood stage at the end of May. Abandoned homes with messages smeared in mud and sprayed in paint seemed addressed to me: "Sightseers GO AWAY," "Stay Out," and "TOURIST ATTRACTION CENTER." Those signs achieved their goal. I felt low. But I returned several more times and stared and tried to feel.

During my first weeks at UND, what I felt was an acute sense of missing out. I lacked the shared experience of returning students; I was not part of this community forged through calamity. That absurd desire for tragic communion, however, would find its way back to me. I would learn firsthand loss and recovery, delayed grief and meaningless guilt.

My mom wrote me 22 letters and sent me 30 emails while I was in college:

"I hope you and your roommates get to be friends so the transition will be easier on all of you. When you drive the car, please be very careful. I don't want you getting hurt! Are there anythings you can think of that we forgot to buy or bring up? You'll have to let me know. I will go for now. Call home whenever you want. Love you bunches! Love, Mom" — letter, September 7, 1996

"Sure enjoyed the weekend with all of us together. Kind of like a little family vacation." — letter, October 7, 1996

"Hope you can get a ride somewhere close for Thanksgiving vacation. Have to let us know." — letter, October 27, 1996

Most of her messages came after she got sick.

"My CAT scan report came back good with no internal organs involved. I had a bone scan today to see how the radiation is doing. I'm feeling much better, getting to be a regular couch potatoe!!" — letter, December 5, 1996

"Hi Toots, I'm learning how to use this e-mail. Not too difficult. Sounds like you have alot of schoolwork! Today is Dad's birthday. You won't miss the cake because its German chocolate." — email, August 30, 1997

"Tomorrow Dad & I go to Paynesville again. I get chemo tomorrow. Sure am glad so happy that its working! Now I'm going to slowly take walks outside & go a little farther everyday. Get my muscles going again. Enough of being a couch potato." — letter, September 22, 1997

"Saturday dad and I might go to an auction in Danvers. I want to look at a bedroom set for our room and get rid of this hospital bed.... Be careful with your body playing volleyball and remember the floor isnt the same as the sand." — letter, September 25, 1997

"Hi Joshua, Well the guy is here installing Primestar. Dad & him are outside deciding where to put the dish. I don't know if I'll be able to figure out the control. I still have problems with our old one. Guess we can tape movies while we are watching them too." — letter, October 15, 1997

"You and Jim please stay awake wed. night. Youll both be relaxed after finals. You both keep each other awake. Not one sleep whiler one drives. See you early thurs morning. Am thinking of you and all your studying.keep up the good work. love you bunches!mom" — email, December 15, 1997

"hi toots, sorry your plans didn't work out as planned....I know you like things organized and to follow your plans but sometimes you have to be flexible. get your christmas spirit back,ok . love you bunches,mom" — email December 16, 1997

"well ur mother had good news at the drs. today.
bonescan showed no new cancer activity
ct scan showed everything to be normal, liver, kidneys, lungs, etc.
mamogram was normal
tumor marker count was well within the normal range
so all that was as good as could be expected, she's going to have a mri on
friday to try and find the cause the cause of the spasams in her shoulder.

saw the dr today and had chemo to day so was a long day and we have to go to
grampas for birthday party tonight…
better go put clothes in the dryer and reload the washer
culdad@" — email, January 13, 1998

During my first two years in Grand Forks, I never encountered a panhandler, and while this woman in the parking lot wasn't asking for money, her forwardness unnerved me. After I agreed to drive her home, she zipped over to the right side of my silver 1986 Chevy Celebrity. I opened the passenger door and aligned her wheelchair parallel with the car seat. I stood behind her, unsure of what to do next. She reached and put a hand on the top of the open door, and then paused.

"Would you mind putting the floor mat on top of the seat?" she asked.

What? Why? I felt insulted.

"Oh no that's okay," I said. "My seat is clean. You can sit on it."

"No, it's just—" she said with a crinkle. "It's just that—sometimes I have accidents." She drew out the first syllable of that last word.

"Sure, yep, no problem," I said. "Let me—" I grabbed the floor mat and quickly shook off the sand and gravel, and then I placed it on top of the passenger seat.

I felt myself once again begin to dissociate. I was acting and talking in the present, but my mind was moving off to some middle distance. I settled into a space independent of my own interiority. I watched myself but I could not make sense of what was going on.

With the floor mat in place, the woman once again grabbed the passenger door with her right arm and began to hydraulic herself up and out of the chair. I placed my hand on her back and steadied her. I tried to guide her as she rolled counterclockwise onto the passenger seat. She landed on the dusty rubber mat with a gasping sigh, and I closed the door.

I did not go through the stations like the rest of my family.

I was only three hours away, but I was absent for most of my mom's sickness. I had class. I had work. I had excuses. I came home for deer hunting and holidays and spring break. Otherwise, I called. I emailed. I stayed away.

When I did come home, my job was distraction. I'd grab her walker and pretend I was a World War II ball-turret gunner. I'd intentionally eat too much supper, then announce to my slightly unnerved family: "I didn't come to paint!" I tried to make everyone feel better, divert them from their sadness. Really, though, I was distracting myself. I turned away rather than confront reality. Guilt is the absence of courage, and cowardice metastasizes. So my mom and I would play cribbage. We'd watch the Food Network. I'd talk.

My mom slept on the couch. Her bed was too high to climb into and too difficult to sit in. So, every night for two years she stretched out on the sofa, and my dad curled into the loveseat beside her. They got satellite television—I'm sure the first in the county to have it. Each night they'd settle in for endless episodes of *Emeril*. The hypnotic glow of the TV and the morphine drip caused my mom to doze off while facing the television. Her head, in repose, fell forward, chin resting on chest. A few years of sleeping like this and she could no longer straighten her neck. When she stood, her torso looked like a bass clef.

On one of my irregular visits home I was horrified by this hunch of a woman. Why couldn't she straighten up. Why couldn't she raise her head? Hadn't anybody noticed? I had an idea—a neck brace! Force her head up, damn the pain. And so she did what I asked. She dutifully donned the neck brace whenever I was around. Only occasionally would she protest when it became too much, when *I* became too much.

"Mom, why aren't you wearing your neck brace?" I'd ask.

"Joshua," she'd say. "It hurts." It was the only time I ever heard resignation in her voice.

When I'd head back to school, they'd put the brace away. Her head would once again bob and fall. After a while, sores developed.

One in the dip between her clavicles, the other underneath her chin. Red and yellow ovals crusted with puss, seeping and suppurating.

At that point, there was nothing to do except keep the wounds clean.

How the fuck do you break down a wheelchair?

I had no idea. I'd never done it before. I stood wondering how to flatten this three-dimensional object so I could slide it into my backseat. The woman in the front offered no help. She sat and talked to herself or talked to me. It wasn't clear. Either way, she wasn't reciting the operating manual.

For five minutes I stood under the streetlamp fiddling with that goddamn chair. Finally, it folded. I opened my back door and was reminded of all the shit in my backseat. I had moved out of my apartment earlier that spring, the way college students turn into nomads every May, lugging their life through the summer until school starts again. In my car was a vacuum cleaner, mop bucket, mop, broom, and a bucket of cleaning supplies. I pulled each piece out and placed it on the pavement. I slid the wheelchair behind the woman's seat then Rubik's cubed everything else back in one-by-one.

I closed the door and walked around the car, then paused. It was 11:30 p.m. There was a stranger in my front seat. A wheelchair bound, possibly incontinent woman sitting on my floor mat in case she pissed herself. I didn't know where she lived, but I was about to drive her home.

I hopped in and put the car in reverse. I reached my right arm behind the passenger seat, checked over my shoulder, and began to back up.

"Can we stop for Weenie Wednesday?" she asked.

I braked, put the car in park. I looked at her, my arm still behind her seat.

"What?" I asked. "What is that?"

"Weenie Wednesday. At this gas station you can stop and on Wednesdays they have hot dogs for 99 cents," she said. "Can we stop and get one?"

"Uh, I don't think so. Not tonight," I said. "Let's just get you home. It's pretty late."

"But I'm hungry and I haven't eaten today and I really want a hot dog and it's Weenie Wednesday!"

"Where do you live?" I asked.

She wouldn't say. Instead, she flung into a fit. I realized she was perhaps developmentally disabled. She pleaded with a toddler's persistence. I caved.

"Okay okay okay, yes, we'll stop and get a hot dog," I said, putting the car into gear and backing out of the parking spot.

My ninth birthday party was the first that included more than just my family members. Because I had a summer birthday, and lived ten miles out of town, after-school celebrations were not a thing. But my mom organized a party for mid-April, when the frost lets out and it's finally fit for a tangle of boys to run wild outside. I passed out her handmade invitations weeks in advance.

After school, a dozen of us set siege on the school bus where we bounced over gravel roads for 45 minutes until the door accordioned open and released us. We raced each other up the fishhook driveway. Anything was possible.

In Reading class earlier that year we had read a short story about a boy who celebrates his birthday with friends by eating hot dogs and watermelon on a bright summer day. That was my theme, and my friends instantly recognized the premise. "This is just like in Reading class!" they said, seemingly in unison, as we congregated in the kitchen. There was a tray of hot dogs in generic white bread buns and quarter moon stacks of watermelon on the island. My mom had also baked a yellow cake with chocolate frosting and hung balloons up in the kitchen and dining room. I think we both felt proud to pull off such a recognizable celebration.

The party, of course, was a disaster. It imploded the way all gatherings of nine-year-olds tend to collapse. Friends fractured into factions. There was in-fighting, hurt feelings. My lasting memory is of my friends, Mike and Jordan, arguing and shoving one another by the patio door. My brother, then a high school senior, stood washing dishes on the other side of the island. Besieged by brats all afternoon he finally burst.

"Hey!" he yelled, "Fuckin' knock it off!" He had a jut of an Adam's apple and a mustache. The two boys froze, then slid open the patio door and slipped out.

Not long after, it was time for everyone to go home. My mom passed out gift baskets to all the boys. Candy and baseball cards wrapped up in tissue paper and tied together with a ribbon. She brought them home in rounds, and I rode shotgun as we crisscrossed the countryside. She drove a hundred miles that night.

I'd like to think that when we got home we sat down at the kitchen island exhausted, but elated.

So did you have a good birthday?

I'd answer between bites of watermelon, spitting seeds into a cereal bowl, gap-toothed smile still not something I was self-conscious about.

Yes! It was the best! Then: *Thank you for all of this.*

But that didn't happen. I was nine and she wasn't yet sick. I'm sure I just grabbed my baseball cards, and maybe a hotdog, and disappeared into my room.

We were silent as we drove down University Avenue. I don't remember if I asked her name; I know she did not ask mine. We turned onto Columbia Road and headed south, cresting the overpass. I looked left at the run-down Burger Time apartments, where I would move at the end of the summer. Then something occurred to me: I had no money. No cash. No checks. No debit card.

As we neared the Valley Dairy on 24th Avenue, I asked the woman if she had any money for the hotdogs.

"Can't you buy it?" she asked.

We crossed traffic and pulled into the convenience store. I parked at the gas pump furthest port side from the entrance, in what was perhaps a subconscious attempt to block her view as I reconnoitered for discount wieners. I scrounged underneath my seat and dug deep into its cushion's crevice for change. Meanwhile, the woman offered a running commentary on my pecuniary safari: "Well you must have *some* money." Exasperated, she searched her purse. Together we came up with $1.35. With this bounty of coins I opened the door, but the woman stopped me with last minute directions.

"Make sure that you get it with mustard, and relish, and ketchup," she said. I paused, and looked at her.

"Sure, yep, I'll make sure I get all that," I said.

Mom mom's great hope was to visit me in Grand Forks. My family had trekked up to Duluth during my first year for "Family Weekend" and she hoped to see my home at this new university as well. And even as her own health fluctuated, she was vigilant about my own.

> *"hi toots, hope your breathing is better, dont let it go to long, go to the student infimary and get some antibiotic that does not contain any penicillin! . Dont let them give you amoxillin! Im having a tough day of breathing myself today, dont know if it's the medicine or if im getting asthma, I dont know how you can tolerate more then a day of being short of breath! Its terrible."* — email, March 25, 1998

> *"I M feeling better too, that not being able to breathe really gets you down and dark under the eyes. Its scary when you cant catch your breath, dangerous! .... What do you want the easter bunny to bring you?"* — email, March 28, 1998

> *"good morning joshua, its a gorgeous day out, sun is shining, dad and tony are out cutting the big tree down....I know I always wanted it*

down for a a three season porch but now when its too late I want it back." — email, April 4, 1998

"I told dad that one weekend in July I want us all to come up & see you & your school. Do you have an open weekend in July?" — letter, June 26, 1998

"Hi Joshua, Hope you have your computer figured out. We are coming up around ~~noon on Sat 18 and coming home Sun 19 around noon. Will be great to see you and where you live & go to school. We will probably bring up the girl's sleeping bags & sleep in chairs or whatever Sat night.~~ *Will talk to you later this week. Love you Bunches Mom.*

Forget about us coming up Sat July 18. Sarah has to work every weekend & can't get off. They are too short staffed! So don't ask for the night off at Apple Bees or at S/A. Really disappointing!! Don't know now when we can come up. Really makes me angry. Talk to you later. Love you Mom!" — letter, July 6, 1998

"good morning Joshua! I dont know what is so good about it. Dont ask for any days off because we cant make it up to see you on July 18 and 19. Sarah has to work every weekend in July and they are too short staffed for her to trade .I dont know when we will be able to come and see you, Really makes me angry." — email, July 7, 1998

"Saw Janine V. in the drugstore the other day and she says hi. Says she has hardly seen you all summer. She isn't the only one." — letter, July 13, 1998

"You see how late you work friday before deciding to come home that night or start out sat. morning which would be a better idea. I dont like you out there alone at night in case you have car problems. I know I worry too much, but I love you!" — email, August 11, 1998

"I had my wbc checked tues and its just about knocked out completely from the chemo drug so now Im going every day till friday to monte

hosp for an injection to stimulate my bone marrrow. Hopefully it will be up by friday and i wont need any more shots." — email, August 26, 1998

"Hi Joshua, Check with your registrar office and see if you have to finish filling in the blanks from direct loans.
How is your week going? My week is OK except for straightening my neck." — letter, September 3, 1998

"sorry we haven't written for awhile but it's been hard to find time even though I haven't worked for two weeks. you're mothers been vary sick so I've had to be here all the time … you're mother is some better now, they determined she wasn't getting enough oxygen so they put her on steroids seems to have helped some….
ur mother says hi and reminded me to tell u about sam, he's been missing for 4 days, don't know what happened but he's never taken off before in ten years so it doesn't look good.
well i've rambled enough for now
culdad@" — email, November 1, 1998

There were no hotdogs. Of course there were no hotdogs!

It was nearly midnight. I asked a guy mopping the floor if there were any franks left from Weenie Wednesday. He looked at me and said nothing. Through the window behind the counter I could see the woman in my car, craning her head over her right shoulder with great distress. She was tracking my progress, making sure I didn't forget the ketchup, mustard, and relish.

I know I had no actual obligation to this woman, but I felt panicked standing there. She expected a hot dog, and I told her I'd get her one. I needed to keep my word. I felt stupidly responsible, and with $1.35 in my sandy pocket, my alternatives were limited. Finally, in the back of the store I saw they had a bin of popcorn. A bag cost a buck and a quarter, so I bought one.

I left Valley Dairy with the popcorn, and a spare dime in my pocket. I walked sheepishly to the car. I opened the passenger door and was met by her expectant eyes.

"Did you get the hot dog?" she asked.

"I'm sorry," I said. "They didn't have any hotdogs inside." Her eyes filled, while her body deflated.

"But I wanted a hot dog!" she cried.

"Yes, I understand that you wanted a hot dog," I said. "But there *were* no hot dogs."

I quickly held out my left hand. "But I got you some popcorn!" I said. She snatched the bag out of my hand, and grabbed a fistful. She was excited to get a treat; it didn't matter what it was. And with the hot dog betrayal behind us, she gave me the remaining directions to her apartment.

It took three minutes to get there. When she saw the building, she pointed and said, "Here it is! Here it is!" I pulled up to the curb and got out while she finished her snack. I opened a back door and repeated the whole belabored routine. Out came the vacuum cleaner. Out came the mop. The broom, the bucket, and finally the wheelchair. I had already forgotten how I flattened it, so I wrestled with that goddamn thing for five minutes to get it street-legal. Meanwhile, she was mined the bag for kernels.

Finally, I got the wheelchair set up, and I rolled it next to the car. She's finished the popcorn and set the bag down on the center console.

"Are you ready?" I asked.

Six months earlier she was alive. One morning, a week before Christmas, I walked into the living room and she was still asleep on the couch. Her head was bowed. Her chin on her chest fusing the open sores. Her strawberry protein drink sat untouched on the table. On the carpet, an empty Blue Bunny ice cream pail where she often returned her breakfast. Her rough cloth turban, which looked like a washcloth, was pushed back revealing her scrubby scalp. There was barely fuzz on her bald head. But she was there.

Then that evening she was gone.

I'd spent Christmas day shopping with my sisters. We sleepwalked through a mall all day, then left in the dark. An hour home through the crystalline night, then that slow turn up the driveway and toward the unknown. There were no cars parked outside, no note inside. We said nothing to each other. Instead, we wrapped presents.

Later someone called. She was in the hospital, in a coma.

We waited. What else was there to do? My dad called every day. There was nothing to update, so instead he'd tell me: "Make sure you don't leave any towels on the goddamn stove." I don't recall anyone ever leaving dish towels on the goddamn stove, but I told him I'd make sure we didn't.

December morning light in Minnesota is slow and filmy. It was three days later and we knew already, but we waited for the car's headlights to puncture that fog. Through the picture window we saw the car pass through the tree line a quarter mile off. We stood for what seemed like hours.

The door opened and my mom's small mom came in first. She was not brave for us or for herself. She was stricken, wordless. My dad followed and closed the door. We stood there in a line extending from the patio door, as if facing a firing squad.

"Well," he said, trailing off. "It's all over."

And there it was. The mass of the past four years, the black hole that consumed everything, collapsed into a single moment. Three words. We didn't move. He walked towards us. Grabbed us, one by one.

"Hug a little bit," he said. "Cry a little bit."

We did.

Sitting outside her home, the woman said she was ready. I thought I was, too. I held the door as she reached her right arm out to grab the top of the window. She braced her left hand hard against the center console; the popcorn bag scrunched beneath it. She pushed herself up with great strain. I placed my left hand on her back to help steady her. As soon as she jacked herself halfway up, she paused.

"Are you okay?" I asked.

She gurgled something unintelligible, and followed it with a gaseous sigh. Then the air soured.

"Ohhh—I'm sorry," she said.

I looked down and the floor mat was filled with urine.

"Oh no that's okay, that's okay," I said. "Let's just get you into your wheelchair and get you inside."

I tried to push her up with my left hand, but she only pitched forward. She grabbed the door tighter with her right hand and pulled herself up and into the wheelchair. She smelled like ammonia, and I tried not to gag. Neither of us said anything as I popped the chair's front wheels up and over the curb. I yanked the back end of her chair up and over the hump. With all four wheels on the same plain she took off, not looking back or saying thank you or goodnight. She rolled straight to her building, keyed in a code, and disappeared inside. I remember it now as happening with a cartoonish quickness.

I turned around in my sandy flip-flops and looked at the car. The car my mom drove us home in after my ninth birthday. The car she let me borrow during my first month of college. The car I drove down to the Red River wreckage. The car now with a front seat full of pee. The desultory vacuum cleaner on the sidewalk. Three car doors were open.

How was I ever going to tell this story?

I should've thrown the goddamn floor mat out right away; left it there on the sidewalk. I should have done a lot of things. Instead, I silently slid the vacuum into the car and closed the doors. I hopped in and rolled down my window. I made a cautious U-turn, before turning right onto Columbia Road and drove home alone.

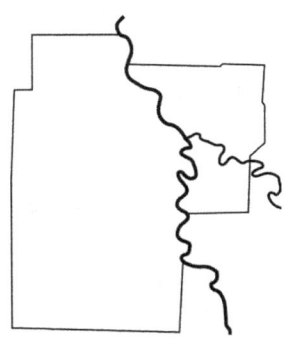

Conversation with Gordon Iseminger

A Fight for History

David Haeselin

Today, many residents of Red River Valley are more than happy to report that the flood of 1997 is behind them; they have mucked out and moved on. For Professor Gordon Iseminger, though, it seems that his body remembers the flood even after his mind has worked so hard to forget.

Professor Iseminger is a dapper chap, with a sense of professorial style from a more civilized age. When I met him in his office, Iseminger was wearing a dark gray suit and a tie with a bold knot. This was my first time meeting him, but I imagine that he never sets foot on campus in anything less. His excitement about history and ideas are palpable, both in his demeanor and his book-cluttered office; Professor Iseminger is most comfortable living the life of the mind. At the beginning of our conversation, he confessed to me that he was not equipped to deal with the physical stress of the flood and recovery. Yet, somehow, like so many other Grand Forksers, he found a way.

At 5 a.m. on April 19, 1997, Professor Iseminger was jolted awake by flood sirens. He quickly woke his wife, and together, they moved everything they possibly could up from their basement. They closed the front door on 9th Ave N and hoped for the best. Iseminger narrates these memories of the event in the language similar to that of Post-Traumatic Stress Disorder (PTSD). He reported to me that he still wakes up nearly every day at 5 a.m. He also explained that he shudders whenever he hears a siren. It cannot be easy to live, as he does, just blocks from a main fire station in Grand Forks.

As UND's longest serving faculty member, Iseminger has witnessed both Grand Forks and the university's growth. At the time of his arrival, Grand Forks was a small, self-contained city, stretching only a few blocks past the historic downtown, with a few condensed neighborhoods scattered around. During these years, Iseminger tried to purchase a home in the Riverside neighborhood, a small neighborhood that contains many historic Craftsman, Victorian, and Tudor Revival style houses. Finding that none were available, he decided to buy in Near North, not far from the University and some two miles from the Red River. In April 1997, "he finally got his wish to live by the river," he joked.

Many Grand Forks leaders were rightly worried about the flood's threat to the population of the city. There was no telling how many people would just pick up and leave if their homes were condemned. The fact that Grand Forks' population returned quickly after the flood and has even grown since, stands as a testament to the decision-making skills and vision of those hard-working people that served the city during its recovery. Grand Forks now boasts nearly sixty-thousand people, more than the years before the flood. In response to this trend, Iseminger said, "I don't know where Grand Forks is going," while adding that Grand Forks recovered "better than expected," and faster, too.

Growth is obviously a major goal of any city, especially one that experienced a historic natural disaster. But during our conversation, Iseminger repeatedly reminded me that this growth often comes at a cost. Most near and dear to him, the push for growth means neglecting to preserve and maintain places of historical interest; once old structures are gone, they are gone forever. Iseminger's fears mirror those of other critics of unregulated urban growth. The argument goes that unplanned development threatens to homogenize all municipalities into carbon copies of one another — generic strips of big-box stores where a visitor feels could be anywhere in the United States. The south end of Grand Forks has become increasingly developed since the flood, and accounts for much of the city's population and commercial growth.

Since 1997, Iseminger has played an active part in the Grand Forks Historic Preservation Committee. Some notable accomplishments include saving some of the most impressive and important structures in the city: St. Michael's Hospital (now Riverside Manor), the Metropolitan Opera House (now the Rhombus Brewing Company), and a landmark rotating train bridge that once crossed the Red between downtown Grand Forks and East Grand; only the foundation of the bridge still stands in the middle of the river, but its importance is explained on a plaque on the East Grand side. What's more, the committee convinced the federal government to recognize the neighborhoods Riverside, Near Southside, Downtown, and the University as historic districts. This recognition has helped keep the look and feel of these historic neighborhoods intact, as well as inspired residents to create active neighborhood associations.

The Historic Preservation Society's successes are not universally lauded, however. Iseminger reported that those on the committee were always seen as troublemakers standing in the way of "wonderful opportunities to build something new." Indeed, historical preservation may not always seem like the most prudent addition on day-to-day decisions. But the justification for much of the preservation society's work was that the flood (and the resultant) fire, disproportionally affected the oldest parts of Grand Forks; not unlike most river towns, Grand Forks' development started at the river and then spiraled outwards from there. The residents of Riverside, and patrons of Rhombus Brewing, myself included on both accounts, are privileged to get to regularly experience history firsthand by living and gathering in places that have stood the test of time.

Perhaps the preservation that matters most to Iseminger is a personal example. His house on 9th Ave N was hit hard in 1997. Floodwaters rose to four feet on his ground floor. Much of what he and his wife had collected over forty years of marriage was destroyed. But the structure was still *his*. He did not want to move even though he had enough money saved to rent an apartment and the city buyout would have probably been enough for him to buy another home. This humble structure mattered to him and to history. It was worth fighting for. And fight he did.

Iseminger spent the entire summer of 1997 mucking out his destroyed basement and first floor, only to be denied a building permit from the city. He was crushed. Iseminger fought the decision. After managing to schedule a final appraisal by the city inspector, Iseminger doubled down; he trimmed the surrounding trees, the hedges, mopped what was left of his floor. Upon the inspector's arrival, Iseminger pleaded: "just look at this place." Even through the rough veneer, the inspector saw the value Iseminger had wanted to show him. Later that day, Iseminger received a call from the city saying that he had been issued a building permit. He could now legally start repairing his home. "To this day, I don't know what that fella did," Iseminger admitted.

Remembering our history, even the epic kind, should not be thought of as a given. Things change as do people. Many, if not most, of the people living in Grand Forks today have no personal connection to the flood. This is partially because the city has grown as have its major employers: the University of North Dakota, the United States Air Force Base outside town in Emerado, and the Altru hospital and medical clinics. North Dakota's remarkably low unemployment rate (3% as of December 2016, fifth lowest in the U.S.) probably has something to do with it as well. Growth and prosperity means newcomers.

Without a sense of history, though, how can these newcomers expect to know their new neighbors? Iseminger complained that "I have never experienced a city that is as little historic minded" as Grand Forks. As for the University of North Dakota, he said that they are determined "to get rid of anything that deals with the history of the university." I hope that Iseminger is wrong about this assessment, but only time will tell.

At the end of our conversation, Iseminger expressed his sincere worry about the future of historical memory in American culture. "I can't expect people to share my enthusiasm for history," he said, "but they don't have to be so obtuse; they don't have to be so antagonistic." I share Iseminger's distaste at this willed amnesia, a sense of progress that willingly paves over the past. But I also think his sense of the public's antagonism could use a bit more context. History can hurt. It often feels like excess baggage. What good is dwelling in the past when we have so many challenges facing us in the future?

Near the end of our conversation, Professor Iseminger offered me wisdom he's gleaned from half a century of teaching and writing: his love of history has sustained him though all of this loss. "I've seen people deal with worse," he said. But this doesn't mean we can afford to forget.

If we forget the flood, we also forget all the hard work it took to help the Red River Valley recover. And if we forget that recovery is possible, we start to doubt that progress, itself, is possible. As Iseminger suggested when successfully making the case to save his own home, "this place is too valuable to be bulldozed into a hole in the ground."

911 Call

We Are Officially Closed

April 18th, 1997, 6:31 am
Call 1356
Transcription and Quality Assurance by
Matthew Nelson

Audio link: https://perma.cc/3GLP-M97P

April 18th, 1997, 6:00 am, City orders evacuation of Riverside and Central Park areas.

Dispatcher: Law enforcement center.
Caller: Hey, it just changed.
Dispatcher: Yeah?
Caller: This is [unintelligible] on the radio, uh...President Baker, now he's saying we're closed.
Dispatcher: For faculty, staff, everybody.
Caller: Yep, and he wants people to volunteer to come and help. But, we are officially closed.
Dispatcher: Okay, thank you!
Caller: Yep.

5
Lessons

This information is being made available to you from the City of Grand Forks so that you are aware of flood hazards to your property. Your questions and comments on the subjects covered here are welcomed and appreciated. To find out more about your property and if it's in the flood hazard area, contact the Inspection Department. The department office is located in City Hall (255 North 4th Street) on the second floor, or you can reach us at 746-2631. The Inspection Department has reference materials on floodplain regulations, floodproofing, and retrofitting. Also, the Grand Forks Public Library has been supplied with an extensive collection of materials on these subjects for your use.

Reference:
City of Grand Forks Flood Preparedness Pamphlet. 1997 OGL #1351, Box 3, Folder 5. Elwyn B. Robinson Department of Special Collections, Chester Fritz Library, University of North Dakota, Grand Forks.

Document:

Floods Do Happen!

City of Grand Forks

This information is being made available to you from the City of Grand Forks so that you are aware of flood hazards to your property. Your questions and comments on the subjects covered here are welcomed and appreciated. To find out more about your property and if it's in the flood hazard area, contact the Inspection Department. The department office is located in City Hall (255 North 4th Street) on the second floor, or you can reach us at 746-2631. The Inspection Department has reference materials on floodplain regulations, floodproofing, and retrofitting. Also, the Grand Forks Public Library has been supplied with an extensive collection of materials on these subjects for your use.

FLOOD SAFETY

There are several actions residents of flood hazard areas can take to decrease the potential of injury due to flooding.

- Know the flood warning procedures and evacuate the flood hazard area when advised to do so.
- Do not attempt to walk through a flooded area.
- Keep children away from flood waters, ditches, culverts, and storm drains.

CITY OF GRAND FORKS 100 YEAR FLOODPLAIN

NOTE: All dimensions, descriptions, measurements, boundaries and data contained in this nonstandard document are included for general information only. No warranties or covenants are made or given by the City of Grand Forks. Any user must confirm the accuracy of the same with official records, and/or by survey.

The 100 year flood line shown on this map was digitized from the official FIRM Map, and is for reference only. Determination as to whether or not a property is within the 100 year flood zone must be made from the Flood Insurance Rate Map as published by the Federal Emergency Management Agency.

FEBRUARY 11, 1998
CITY ENGINEER: KENNETH A. VEIN
THIS MAP IS COMPUTER DRAWN BY THE CITY OF GRAND FORKS ENGINEERING DEPARTMENT

- - - - 100 Year Floodplain
——— City Limits

THE FLOOD HAZARD

The Grand Forks - East Grand Forks urban area is located on the flat floodplain at the junction of the Red River of the North and Red Lake River. Although this location met early development needs for transportation routes, power, and water supplies, it leaves residents of Grand Forks vulnerable to periodic economic losses and threats to public health and safety from floods. Existing permanent and emergency flood barriers and non-structural measures such as flood insurance, floodplain regulations, flood forecasts and warnings, and floodproofing have helped to reduce flood losses and threats to public health and safety.

Principal factors contributing to flooding at Grand Forks include the very flat river slope; northward drainage into still frozen reaches, channel obstructions and, to some extent, increasing agricultural drainage. The area is subject to spring snowmelt and summer thunderstorm flooding of the Red River of the North and flash flooding along the English Coulee at any time. Records of river flooding have been maintained since 1882. These measurements have been recorded by the U.S. Geological Survey gauge. This gauge has been moved several times over the years; it is presently located at River Mile 297.6, just south of the Sorlie Bridge on DeMers Avenue. The bottom of the river channel at that location is River Gauge 0.0 or 779.0 feet above mean sea level. Flood stage in Grand Forks is at 28 feet (River Gauge) or 807.0 (M.S.L.). The April 1997 flood reached a river gauge of 54.11 feet or 833.11 M.S.L. with a corresponding return interval of about 210 years. A return interval of once every 100 years, or a one-percent chance of flood, would have to reach a river stage of 52.0 feet or a M.S.L. elevation of 831.0 feet.

THE FLOOD HAZARD

The Grand Forks - East Grand Forks urban area is located on the flat floodplain at the junction of the Red River of the North and Red Lake River. Although this location met early development needs for transportation routes, power, and water supplies, it leaves residents of Grand Forks vulnerable to periodic economic losses and threats to public health and safety from floods. Existing permanent and emergency flood barriers and non-structural measures such as flood insurance, floodplain regulations, flood forecasts and warnings, and floodproofing have helped to reduce flood losses and threats to public health and safety.

Principal factors contributing to flooding at Grand Forks include the very flat river slope; northward drainage into still frozen reaches; channel obstructions and, to some extent, increasing agricultural drainage. The area is subject to spring snowmelt and summer thunderstorm flooding of the Red River of the North and flash flooding along the English Coulee at any time. Records of river flooding have been maintained since 1882. These measurements have been recorded by the U.S. Geological Survey gauge. This gauge has been moved several times over the years; it is presently located at River Mile 297.6, just south of the Sorlie Bridge on DeMers Avenue. The bottom of the river channel at thal location is River Gauge 0.0 or 779.0 feet above mean sea level. Flood stage in Grand Forks is at 28 feet (River Gauge) or 807.0 (M.S.L.). The April 1997 flood reached a river gauge of 54.11 feet or 833.11 M.S.L. with a corresponding return interval of about 210 years. A return interval of once every 100 years, or a one-percent chance of flood, would have to reach a river stage of 52.0 feet or a M.S.L. elevation of 831.0 feet.

- Do not drive through a flooded area or around road barriers; the road may be washed out.
- If your vehicle stalls in high water, abandon it immediately and seek higher ground.
- Have your electricity turned off by the Power Company or cut off all electric circuits at the fuse panel or disconnect switches. Stay away from power lines and electric wires.
- If this is not possible, turn off or disconnect all electrical appliances. Don't use appliances or motors that have gotten wet unless they have been taken apart, cleaned, and dried.
- Shut off the water services and gas valves in your home.
- Look out for animals.
- Look before you step. After a flood, the ground and floors are covered with debris and mud and can be very slippery.
- Be alert for gas leaks. Use a flashlight to inspect for damage. Don't smoke or use candles, lanterns, or open flames unless you know the gas has been turned off and the area has been ventilated.
- Use a generator or other gasoline-powered machine outdoors only, as they can produce dangerous levels of Carbon Monoxide (CO).

Clean everything that got wet. Flood waters may have picked up sewage and chemicals from roads, farms, factories, and storage buildings. Spoiled food, flooded cosmetics, and medicine can be health hazards. When in doubt, throw them out.

FLOOD WARNING SYSTEM

The Grand Forks Emergency Operation Plan provides comprehensive procedures for preflood preparations, emergency flood response, evacuation and disaster relief activities, and postflood activities. The plan sets forth the criteria and procedures for initiating and conducting a flood response, and the organizational structure and coordinated mechanisms required between all levels of government and the public.

The Emergency Operation Center (EOC) provides a central location and facility for control, coordination, and communications in response to a flood emergency. The EOC is located in the basement of the police building (122 South 5th Street, Room 21). It provides facilities for command/communication functions, meetings and conferences, and for preparing public information releases. Flood forecasts are issued by the National Weather Service. The activation of the EOC will depend on the forecasted crest at Grand Forks.

Stay tuned to local radio or local TV stations, and also to NOAA weather radio for information and updates on flood watches or warnings. The City of Grand Forks has an outdoor warning system that consists of sirens strategically located throughout Grand Forks. The sirens are activated to alert residents to receive the warning message by tuning into local radio or TV stations. Know the terms used to describe flooding:

Flood Watch: Flooding is possible.
Flood Warning: Flooding is occurring or will occur soon.

The Emergency Management Office and Emergency Operation Center can be reached by the public at the following telephone numbers: 701-780-8213 and 701-746-2685 respectively.

PROPERTY PROTECTION MEASURES

Rather than wait for a code requirement, you can act now to protect your property from flood damage. There are various actions which can be taken to retrofit or floodproof structures. Electrical panel boxes, furnaces, water heaters, and washers/dryers should be elevated or relocated to a location less likely to be flooded. Basement valves can be installed, and interior floodwalls can be placed around utilities. Several retrofitting measures include:

- Elevating the building so that flood waters don't enter or reach any damageable portions of it
- Constructing barriers out of fill or concrete between the building and flood waters

- "Dry floodproofing" to make the building walls and floor watertight so water does not enter
- "Wet floodproofing" to modify the structure and relocate the contents so that when flood waters enter the building there is little or no damage, and
- Preventing basement flooding from sewer backup or sump pump failure.

If flooding is likely, and time permits, move essential items and furniture to the upper floors of your home. Keep materials like sandbags, plywood, plastic sheeting, and lumber handy for emergency waterproofing. This action will help minimize the amount of damage caused by floodwaters.

FLOOD INSURANCE

Standard homeowner's insurance policies do not cover losses due to floods. However, Grand Forks is a participant in the National Flood Insurance Program, which makes it possible for Grand Forks property owners to obtain federally backed flood insurance. This insurance is available to any owner of insurable property (a building or its contents) in Grand Forks. Tenants may also insure their personal property against flood loss. Your local insurance agent can sell a separate flood insurance policy under rules and rates set by the Federal government. Any agent can sell a policy, and all agents must charge the same rates. Your rates will not change just because you file a damage claim; they are set on a national basis.

Most people have purchased flood insurance because it was required by the bank with a federally backed mortgage or home improvement loan. You do not need to have a mortgage or live in a SFHA (Special Flood Hazard Area) in order to purchase flood insurance. Usually these policies just cover the building's structure and not the contents. During the kind of flooding that happens in Grand Forks, there is usually more damage to the furniture and contents than there is to the structure. Don't wait for the next flood to buy insurance protection. There is a thirty (30) day waiting period before National Flood Insurance coverage takes effect. Contact your insurance agent for more information or rates and coverage.

DRAINAGE MANAGEMENT SYSTEM

Do not dump or throw anything into the ditches, coulees, rivers, or other bodies of water. Dumping is a violation of Grand Forks City Ordinances. A plugged channel can not carry water, and when it rains, the water has to go somewhere. Every piece of trash can contribute to flooding. Even grass clippings and branches can accumulate and plug channels. If your property is next to a body of water, please do your part and keep the banks clear of brush and debris. The City has a storm drainage system, which is composed of both open and closed segments. The open sections are drainage swales/ditches which are utilized to carry storm waters away from homes to drainage areas such as coulees or rivers. The closed system is comprised of storm water inlets and piping which also carry the water from streets and developments to drainage areas.

Maintenance of the drainage system is very important so that a high flood flow capacity can be realized. To aid in this, the City of Grand Forks clears and performs other maintenance work on the system. Work is also performed on an emergency basis as needed. Debris in ditches obstructs the flow of water and can partially or completely fill in ditches, which can reduce the flood flow capacity and will also result in overflow onto roads and/or private property.

If you see dumping or debris in any body of water, or if you know of any nonapproved changes occurring to the draining system, such as the filling or rerouting of streams or ditches, or a nuisance situation which exists, please contact the Inspection Department at 746-2631.

SUBSTANTIAL IMPROVEMENT REQUIREMENTS

Always check with the Inspection Department before you build on, alter, regrade, or fill on your property. A permit is needed to ensure that projects do not cause problems on other properties. If you see construction without a City permit posted, contact the Inspection Department at 746-2631.

New buildings in the floodplain must be protected from flood damage. Our building code requires that new buildings constructed in the floodplain must be elevated above the base of "100-year" flood elevation. No construction, including filling, can be allowed in the mapped floodway of Grand Forks without an engineering analysis that proves that the project will not increase flood damage elsewhere. The ordinance also requires that all substantial improvements to a building be treated as a new building. A substantial improvement is when the value of an addition, alteration, or reconstruction project exceeds 50% of the value of the existing building.

NATURAL AND BENEFICIAL FLOOD PLAIN FUNCTIONS

Our floodplain plays a valuable part in providing natural and beneficial functions to the area. Floodplains that are relatively undisturbed, or have been restored to a nearly natural state, provide a wide range of benefits to both human and natural systems. These benefits can take many forms: some provide aesthetic pleasure and others function to provide active processes, like filtering nutrients.

Our community has areas of its floodplain that are in a mostly undisturbed state and serve as a natural filtration system, as well as providing flood and erosion control and wildlife habitats. Several of our other floodplain areas are used for recreational purposes as our bike paths and parks along the river (Riverside, Central and Sunbeam Parks). These natural and beneficial functions are not always easily recognized. Here is a short list of some:

- Provide flood water storage and conveyance
- Filter nutrients and impurities from runoff
- Provide open space for aesthetic pleasure
- Maintain bio-diversity and ecosystem integrity

- Contain historic and archaeological sites and provide opportunities for studies
- Provide natural flood and erosion control and reduce flood velocities and peaks
- Create and enhance waterfowl, fish, and other wildlife habitats and provide breeding and feeding grounds

FLOOD PLAIN DEVELOPMENT REGULATIONS

The City of Grand Forks has adopted, as part of the City Code, regulations on the development in flood districts. These regulations specify two types of flood hazard areas: The floodway and the flood fringe. These areas are identified on the map included herein.

The purpose of these regulations is to control alteration of natural floodplains; prevent or regulate the construction of flood barriers which will unnaturally divert flood waters or which may increase flood hazards in other areas; restrict or prohibit uses which may result in damaging increases in erosion or in flood heights or velocities; and to control filling, grading, dredging, and other development which may increase flood damages. Floodplain development permits are required for construction or substantial improvements in flood hazard areas.

Uses which have a low flood damage potential and do not restrict flood flows shall be permitted in the floodway, providing they are not prohibited by another ordinance. These uses shall not require structures, fill, dumping of material or waste, or storage of materials or equipment. The most common uses of the floodway are agricultural or recreational in nature, and parking/lawn areas of residences. Flood fringe districts permit the same types of uses as floodway districts. The construction of structures is also permitted, provided the lowest floor of any structure (which is the basement or main floor if no basement is constructed) is no lower than the base flood elevation.

Grand Forks Flood Disaster and Recovery Lessons Learned

Grand Forks, North Dakota
2011

Prepared by the City of Grand Forks, North Dakota

June 2011

Reference:
City of Grand Forks, North Dakota, "Grand Forks Flood Disaser Recovery Lessons Learned." Accessed on April 13, 2017.
https://perma.cc/5BLA-3ARD

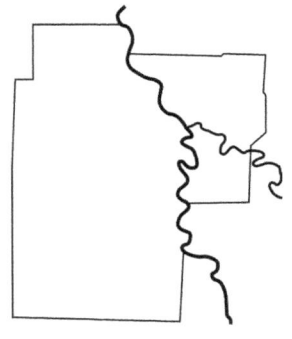

Document:

Grand Forks Flood Disaster and Recovery: Lessons Learned

Prepared by the City of Grand Forks, North Dakota. June 2011

STATEMENT OF INTENT

The City of Grand Forks, North Dakota, would like to take this opportunity to provide a set of local observations garnered during the recovery from our devastating flood that occurred in the Spring of 1997.

We know that all disasters are unique. So are the recoveries. The information presented here may or may not have relevance to your particular situations. However, everyone here stands ready to assist in any way possible whether your call comes tomorrow, next week, or years from now.

The purpose of this material is also to introduce the Grand Forks community to you and convey a message of hope. This message is that although the recovery may be long and often trying, there is a nation behind you, and you will recover.

Sincerely,
Michael R. Brown, Mayor
City of Grand Forks, ND

GRAND FORKS FLOOD RECOVERY BRIEF

In the Spring of 1997, the community of Grand Forks, North Dakota, along with communities all along the Red River Valley, experienced an unprecedented flood with disastrous results.

With over 130,000 cubic feet/second of water raging through the heart of the community, the Red River swelled to over 54.35 feet, overtopped existing levees and surged through the city's infrastructure. Adding to the unbelievable nature of the devastation, a fire broke out in the heart of downtown Grand Forks, consuming 13 buildings as fire fighters battled the blaze from the sky and from the flooded streets.

In this community of 52,500 people, over 90% of the population was evacuated and approximately 12,000 residential and commercial properties were damaged.

There were 13 days without running water and 23 days without potable water. Three quarters of our 40-plus sanitary lift stations were inundated and extensive damage was sustained to our sewer collection system. In financial terms, alone, with over $1.5 Billion in damages, this was a disaster of extreme proportions.

There was heartache and tragedy that had to be addressed. Homes, personal belongings and family businesses were severely affected and, sometimes lost. Over 800 residences had to be removed either because of flood damage or to make way for increased flood protection. Businesses sustained uninsured losses and faced the hard choice of whether to return. In the end, 60,000 tons of debris was hauled away from the homes and businesses that were besieged by floodwaters.

The recovery of this community still continues, but there have been monumental strides taken. Today, a $400 M flood protection project is complete and the population that had dropped by over 3,000 has not only stabilized but has regained pre-flood levels.

Residential and commercial investment in the community, very uncertain in the early months, has surpassed pre-flood levels and the opportunities sought out by residents and the local, state and federal leaders have instilled a reinvigorated life into the community.

More than anything, the support of the Nation kept the candle of hope burning, even in the darkest days. For that, the people of Grand Forks will be forever grateful.

LESSONS LEARNED:
GRAND FORKS 1997 FLOOD RECOVERY

(This is a working document and will be adjusted to reflect on-going circumstances.)

FEDERAL LEADERSHIP

Challenge/Encourage legislators (Federal and State) to figure out ways to streamline regulations such as bidding procedures and resources procurement.

This means either loosening or waiving regulations that will add time or complexity to rebuilding efforts. In addition, flexibility is needed to try to keep the contracts local. Circulating dollars throughout the community are some of the most beneficial recovery tools.

This also means encouraging federal action that will permit agencies to act outside of their normal scope of responsibility. Federal agencies are fundamentally designed to be "stovepipes" and act only within a specific purview. Action outside of this purview is necessary to address the fluid needs of recovery.

WORKING PARTNERSHIP WITH ALL LEVELS OF GOVERNMENT

Great relationships are developed, not expected.
It is absolutely essential that solid partnerships exist between all agencies and on all levels. Recovery is a team effort that relies on the diverse resources and expertise of all parties and "turf wars" must be set aside.

Working with representatives "on the ground."
- **Governor should designate a State Recovery Coordinator to cut through State red tape.**

- **Federal representatives- HUD, FEMA, . . . should work shoulder to shoulder**
  This will give the agencies a greater sense of ownership of the community's recovery needs and mission
- **"Been there, done that" experience is cliché but extremely valuable.**
  Government officials will be able to tell local responders and political leaders what to expect during recovery. They will provide
- **Review decisions made by representatives and get policy decisions in writing.**
  They are caring people dedicated to providing the maximum assistance possible. The result, in some cases is a tendency to say "do what needs to be done" in the immediate aftermath. However, auditors months or years later will have a different attitude. Get decisions in writing so resulting actions can be supported.

Working with Federal and State Agencies in general
- **Establish points of contacts in state and federal agencies and a liaison to work with each.**
  This is imperative to knowing policies as well as the differences that may exist between different districts and jurisdictions (as well as working to minimize these differences) Examples include different policies or interpretations of policies that come from different US Army Corps of Engineers Districts or FEMA districts.
- **It is the local staff/official job to insure federal officials understand local codes and policies**
  A city needs to become a leader and self-directed when it comes to being knowledgeable regarding Federal rules and regulations.
- **Document everything – too much information is enough**
  Document all files and actions, e.g., Damage Survey Reports (DSR) files meticulously
- **Plan for when the city assumes full control**

FEMA will provide absolutely necessary assistance and leadership for varying time periods but each community has to plan for the time in the recovery process to proceed independently.
- **Hire/designate someone to keep up with programs and guidelines and being specific liaison to FEMA, HUD, EDA, USACE**
Designate someone to carefully monitor checklists for all federal and state funds and programs.
- **Clarify Insurance Policies (Was it flood, wind or sewer backup)**

RECOVERY STRUCTURE & PLANNING

- **Put in place a solid Recovery Structure**
Work with federal resources to either hire experts to lead the recovery planning or hire a recovery coordinator or both.
- **A Recovery Plan and Mission is Critical**
A recovery plan keeps elected officials, federal assistance and community members focused on a goal- or phased sets of goals and helps to overcome the day to day hurdles.
- **Impacts of Immediate Action to Long-Range Community Land Use**
The land use decisions made in the next 18 months will have an impact on the community's growth pattern for decades.
- **Mitigation Planning**
It is never to early to learn from the disaster and mitigate future disasters through thoughtful planning
- **Importance of Phased approach to recovery**
A recovery plan should include various phases, i.e., Response, Short Term, Medium Term, Long Term Planning. This allows decision makers to focus time and resources appropriately while establishing clear expectations for citizens.
- **Involve Elected Officials and Citizens, not just "experts" or consultants.**

Elected Officials will have to make the end decisions so they need to know all aspects of the situations. Similarly, citizens need to have ownership. It is their city that is being rebuilt. (See citizen involvement.)

- **Include Non-Profits in the planning**
  Their specialty is working with populations that are often overlooked. Overlooking them in recovery planning will exacerbate existing discrepancies and create new ones.
- **In the end, decisions will have to be made by the decision makers.**
  Decision makers will be held accountable and therefore must remember that their actions are the ones that will define the success or failure of recovery. Their decisions will not always be in full accordance with the expert's opinions and will not always be in full accordance with community members. Which leads to . . .

POLITICS OF LEADERSHIP

- **Political Fallout – Some leaders will not survive**
  Extremely difficult and oftentimes unpopular decisions will have to be made. As an elected official or staff member, it is a time to either make a difference or watch out for your own political life or public career. Upheaval will happen no matter how hard you try to avoid it. Make the RIGHT decisions.

CITIZEN COMMITTEES/INVOLVEMENT

- **Creation of Leadership Teams**
  Grand Forks created several citizen-led leadership teams such as the Business Redevelopment Task Force, Housing Task Force and Downtown Task Force. This encouraged ownership of citizens, businesses and other community organizations.
- **Utilize public forums and charettes**

The city of Grand Forks conducted a charette to "re-imagine Downtown". The end result wasn't exactly as the two-day exercise pictured, but the general character and components were consistent with the direction formed from the dozens of community members who participated. These visions and directions are crucial to policy makers as they make decisions as well as for maintaining cohesive community support for actions.

- **Decisions will take painfully long to make and will happen too quickly**
This paradox demonstrates the public who are waiting for action will feel like decisions are being avoided or being prolonged. Once decisions are made, however, there will be groups who feel they did not have the proper input and they were therefore made hastily. People will be focused on their own concerns for a majority of the time and will not know that seemingly unrelated decisions will have personal impact. Promoting continual and repetitive community discussion can help to address this.

FINANCIAL LESSONS

- **Establish a line of credit for the city**
If the city can't make payments/payroll, what hope does a small business or a family have? The city of Grand Forks, through the assistance of the Governor and the designated State Flood Recovery Coordinator, acquired a $25 M line of credit to ensure bills would be paid in the initial stages while typical income – fees, sales tax and property tax – was not being collected.

- **Impact on Wages and Reemployment**
Wages may rise with influx of recovery jobs paying higher salary. This community experienced an approximate $1/hr increase in many areas of employment.
FEMA employed many local people to fill their needs that ultimately depleted the local workforce and hampered businesses in re-establishing themselves.

- **Economic Effect on Secondary Markets**
  It may seem obvious, but the cost of building supplies, appliances and other secondary market items will increase and the availability will decrease. Citizens are the ones who deal with these increases firsthand and they may feel like gouging. (Although real gouging is a threat that should be guarded against.)
- **Dedicate people to be accountable for every dollar spent.**
  Recovery spending will be scrutinized by granting agencies, citizens and the country.

VOLUNTEERS AND DONATIONS

- **One-Stop Shop for Non-Profits/Service Providers**
  After our flood many local nonprofits, as well as some national nonprofit organizations (that came to town to assist us in the recovery) provided assistance to families. It soon became clear to all of us that 1) families were going from one organization to another in search of help which only added to the confusion and, 2) the various nonprofit organizations had expertise in certain areas but, the average family didn't know that, or where to turn.

  United Way, which does not usually provide direct service to individual clients became a clearinghouse for these requests. All nonprofit organizations (except the Red Cross which had to use their own forms) agreed to one common form that could be filled out at any of the organizations. United Way then entered the information into a central data base (clients had to sign off on the sharing of information). Many times a client was confused about who was actually providing them help, so having one central location to call eased some of the frustration.

  In the beginning, the agencies providing help met almost daily & passed around the requests depending on who had either available resources and/or workers to help out. After the initial weeks, these meetings went to weekly and then finally monthly. We processed over 3,000 cases and the last one was closed out 2 years after the flood.

- **Distribution of Donated Goods**

  Pay strict attention to in-processing, storage, maintenance and delivery of all donations. There will be scrutiny of how things are handled and distributed and the long-term credibility of leadership is at stake.

  United Way also assisted with the distribution of donated goods that came into the community. The city asked us to staff three centers were all of the donated goods that came pouring into Grand Forks were distributed. We had to 1) make sure that individuals were actually living in Grand Forks or East Grand Forks – used drivers licenses first & then asked for FEMA # when we realized that people were simply "shopping" for Christmas Gifts etc. (Remember, besides some of the junk ... used clothes etc., we received things like Microwaves, & other small appliances, clothing from places like Nike etc. 2) Then we had to police things, like people coming in & demanding that they really needed the three microwaves etc.

REBUILDING REGULATIONS

- **"One-Cop Shop"**

  Following the 1997 flood in Grand Forks, North Dakota, city and state officials established, through a joint effort, a one stop shop within the City of Grand Forks for the issuance of state and local transient merchant and contractor licenses. In addition, photo ID's were provided for contractors and contractor employees. Any contractor seeking to provide flood repair or cleanup services in Grand Forks was required to be processed through the one stop shop and obtain photo ID's. All employees of the contractors were also required to have individual picture ID's. Both the contractor and contractor employees were required to possess their photo ID's with them at all times while working within the City. The purpose of the one stop shop was to

coordinate and expedite licensing procedures. The agencies involved included the North Dakota Secretary of State's Office, the North Dakota Office of Attorney General, the North Dakota Workers Compensation Bureau, the North Dakota Bureau of Criminal Investigations, and the Grand Forks Department of Administration and Licensing. Additional assistance and staffing was provided by the Air Guard Security Forces.

Contractors or individuals seeking licenses were required to pay fees, file bonding information, obtain workers compensation coverage, obtain unemployment insurance coverage, and go through a criminal background check in the course of making application for state and local licenses. In addition, they were required to obtain photo identification documents. The one stop shop was located at the Regional North Dakota Job Service Center located in Grand Forks. Criminal background checks were completed on all persons seeking photo identification. More than 20 arrests were made as a result of background checks revealing outstanding warrants. The one stop shop opened on Sunday, April 27, 1997 and remained open until Thursday, July 3, 1997. Thereafter, the City continued its licensing locally and the State resumed its normal licensing operations at the State Capitol in Bismarck. While the one stop shop was in operation, 544 new contractors were licensed and more than 2,400 identification cards were issued to employees of these contractors.

The one stop shop was established despite the fact that there were no sewer or water services in place. The successful operation of the one stop shop was directly related to efforts of employees and cooperation among the respective agencies involved. It is believed that the one stop shop expedited licensing for contractors and their employees to begin helping those in need and in serving as a first line of protection for consumer fraud. It is believed that the one stop shop was successful in discouraging contractors with less than honorable intentions from attempting to do business in the City of Grand Forks. Other benefits included licensing, fee and tax collection, worker protection, consumer protection, business protection, and unemployment insurance.

INFRASTRUCTURE RECOVERY PLANNING

- **Leverage Federal resources with local ones for long-term investment**
  A city needs to leverage the Federal Government's investment to automate and improve the efficiency of the city operation. The vision of the city should be to make investments to make the city better in the long term, which will make the respective state and nation stronger. For example, FEMA will pay to replace the equivalent system, but a city can invest to further upgrade its systems. A public works example is FEMA agreed to pay to replace flooded water meters with an equivalent system and the City of Grand Forks paid for the incremental cost to upgrade and automate the water meter system.

COMMUNICATIONS

- Consistent and Repetitive Communication
  Local governments cannot communicate too much, only too diffusely. This also goes for messages from different entities and agencies. Citizens are sponges soaking up life-changing information and will either seek out or otherwise find contradictory information if it is available. Consistent and repetitive communication is key to ensuring ongoing progress as well as managing expectations. There will be Public Information Officers (PIO) for every conceivable organization working on the disaster. At some point in time they need to have regularly scheduling meetings amongst themselves to ensure:

- Each are getting their message across effectively and consistently
- They can cross-pollinate their messages to increase public awareness
- Sharing of resources

Close monitoring of all major media outlets is important in controlling numerous rumors, speculation, and innuendo long into the recovery stage. The most difficult Public Information Officer work really begins during recovery. Daily reports, pamphlets, newsletters and media articles need to be produced to educate the public on a variety of subjects.

Prior to the flood, the City of Grand Forks had no specific communications department. That office, the Public Information Center, was developed to help with direct communication with the public. Among other things, the Public Information Center began sending a weekly newsletter to residents who were housed in FEMA trailers and also developed a monthly newsletter, called Recovery Road and later Forks Focus, and sent it to approximately 22,000 homes and apartments for approximately two years.

- **Acknowledge Change is necessary and is inevitable – a "New Normal"**
  Repeated the message that there will be a "new normal" where lives will never be exactly the same. People will not be made whole and neighborhoods will never be the mirror image of pre-disaster.
- **Ward Officers**
  Local neighborhood groups and individuals will demand answers and solutions to their problems, many of which will involve potential for civil disorder. The GFPD instituted a Community Policing effort by creating Neighborhood Resource Officers (NROs). These police officers were assigned to and worked in concert with local councilpersons within each council ward/precinct to face and successfully resolve problems in effected areas.
- **Keep the nation informed**

The National media will eventually fade away – with the exception of anniversaries - but people around the country – and world - have placed you in their hearts and will want to know how you're doing

- **Consider hiring historian/anthropologist**
  Firsthand observations come only once and the opportunity to compile an objective view of recovery and chronology of process has already begun

- **IT Infrastructure**
  Be selective in document restoration. The tendency was to restore everything which was unnecessary and very costly. Be aware that accessing the restored documents can cause individuals to have allergic reactions and the restored documents are often hard to read. FEMA allowed us to put scanning systems in place, which makes the documents available both internally and externally. Also, time was spent on restoring hard drives of PC's and only a very few were needed.

  Take the opportunity to setup databases that will work across departments and across agencies. The ability to be able to share the information will help to create efficiencies in government that were almost impossible to achieve when legacy systems were in place. For example, inspection, assessing, lift station information, and pictures of streets are now available to all city departments.

  Find people within the organization who are familiar with computers and the operations in several departments and assign those people to work with IT staff to setup databases, spreadsheets, and other computer applications. As frustrations and tension is high, communications between techies and users can be at an all time high. Having the liaisons work with IT and the various departments can greatly assist in communications.

HOUSING - REBUILDING

- **Rebuilding Residential Neighborhoods (How to replace "Affordable Housing")**
- **Creativity with Community Development Block Grants (CDBG) –**
  It is critical to meet the needs of the people and not simply administer the programs as they were developed years ago in areas far away from the communities where they are now needed. This is also where it is essential to have personal and on-the-ground contact with government agencies so documented policy changes can happen to meet this need.
- **Housing – Using a non-profit entity when private developers are hesitant**
  The Grand Forks Housing Authority is a non-profit, public sector entity that was utilized to spur redevelopment in affordable housing in the early stages where it was generally regarded as risky by private developers.

PERSONNEL ISSUES (STAFFING)

- **Staffing Plan – Use Experts to develop one**
  UTILIZING HUD/CDBG STAFFING NEEDS ASSESSMENT AND MAKING IT FIT THE NEEDS OF THE CITY OF GRAND FORKS

  As time elapsed and the City transitioned from response to recovery, some employees returned to their "normal" government activities, others became extensively immersed in disaster-related activities.

  Recovery placed tremendous pressure of City personnel resources, authorized for normal, non-disaster delivery of public services and government business. The redirection of City personnel to flood aftermath and recovery demands substantially increased the backlog of City departments.

  Adoption of a First Season of Recovery Action Plan which identified goals, objectives and tasks required to maintain flood disaster recovery efforts.

The Mayor requested an assessment be undertaken by HUD/ICF consultants who met with each Department Head in the City to identify staffing needs with regard to flood recovery.

CDBG set aside money for administration from the total allotment of CDBG grant money was used and staffing administration costs were projected for a 3-4 year period of recovery.

Hiring of additional personnel through temporary one-year contracts, the City was able to maintain adequate levels of public services and effectively manage recovery operations which would have been in serious jeopardy had City staff not been available. Importance of having HR staff committed solely to flood recovery hiring processes, including coordination with State job agency and closely monitoring staffing needs on an on-going basis, meeting quarterly with the Department Heads and Mayor to discuss existing flood related projects/programs with relation to staffing. Approximately 3 years was necessary to delegate flood related duties back to existing permanent municipal staff and reviewing the need for permanent staffing additions on an ongoing basis. This process provided the most efficient and cost saving approach to staffing for the public interest. On-going evaluation and communication being key to the entire recovery effort by local government.

- **Take care of your staff!**
EMPLOYEES ARE MOST VALUABLE ASSET FOR RECOVERY EFFORTS

Employees worked to get City up and running and placed their own personal recovery last. A critical need for the quick recovery of a city is to return critical public works infrastructure, such as water and wastewater systems, back to normal operations. A key component in the return is getting city operators back to work to return the critical systems back to normal operation. Professional expertise from engineering consultants and federal agencies (COE and FEMA) is important but does not replace the knowledge and expertise of city operators.

MAYOR ISSUED ADMINISTRATIVE LEAVE FOR TWO WEEK PERIOD IMMEDIATELY FOLLOWING EVACUATION – Salaries continued to be paid for two week period, payroll checks were processed and direct deposited into existing bank accounts. Employees did not miss out on wages or a payday.

EMPLOYEES RELIED ON EMPLOYER FOR SUPPORT AND DIRECTION
- Flexible/Reduced work hours were accommodated by Department Heads at their discretion, for items such as locating family/friends, time for FEMA/SBA appointments, childcare issues, emotional issues, etc. as the City Code had been suspended and the Mayor had full authority.
- Crisis Counseling
- Employee Assistance Program
- On-Call Psychologist Available to City staff
- Inter-Departmental Round Table Discussions held.

- **Awareness of the psychological effects and impact** personal loss would cause thereby affecting their performance as public employees.
- **Importance of having a back up system for payroll and personnel files** for all City employees including retired employees and having that available from an off-site location.
- **Who Helps the First Responders (And City Workers)?** Many first responders will be victims themselves in a large-scale disaster. All Public Safety employees need to have extensive training in the area of Emergency Management/Homeland Security. They especially need to "pre-stage" their own needs and well as the needs of their families in order to remain on the job. City, county and state official must make this a priority to ensure Public Safety is

adequately staffed during a disaster and well into recovery. We experienced:
- Public Safety employees that refused to report to duty until they felt their own families were taken care of first.
- Public Safety administrators that simply had a difficult time dealing with the enormity of the disaster and thus rendered themselves ineffective.
- Public Safety first and second line supervisors that felt this was their time to take over and exhibited too much of a General Patton mentality.

General Murray Sagsveen Army National Guard (and designated by the governor as State Coordinator of the Recovery) was given the responsibility to oversee and co-ordinate all the of the Public Safety groups responding to our disaster which proved to be valuable for objectiveness and overall control functions. He provided a focus on goals and priorities.
- Some will perform amazingly, some will fall apart
- They will have much more pressure than they signed up for
- Bring in assistance to recognize and deal with stress

BUSINESS RECOVERY

- **Establish Planning Committee**
  Made up of business people, citizens and community leaders, a broad-based committee will be essential to achieve both a wide range of suggestions and general support and acceptance.
- **Daycare – Letting people get back to work**
  Our flood happened towards the end of the school year and thus schools simply closed. For that first month afterwards, I don't believe there were any child care facilities even open. Many of the Centers had received damage, as well as the homecare providers. This meant that parents had no safe place to leave their children for the day & thus they did not immediately go back to work. It is important to note here

that North Dakota ranks No. 1 in the number of two parent income families.

Thus, to get people back to work, (especially women who worked as bank tellers, grocery store workers, sales clerks, wait staff etc.) we needed to have safe places for children to be during the day. United Way provided $100,000 to the Park District which set up free daycare throughout the community. To help staff this, child care workers from the centers that were not "up & running" were hired. Also, all of these centers had to then replace equipment & toys that were destroyed in the flood.

- **Taking Too Much** – How much in loans do businesses and residents need?
Many small businesses felt compelled to take out as many loans as possible (as were offered) thinking that it was the cheapest money available (including rumors about forgiving the loans.) In three to five years this debt was too much to handle and hampered the long-term business recovery.
  - **Provide lists of technical assistance and one-on-one advisors** on financial planning (they should be able to determine if they can repay loans.)

ESSENTIAL INFRASTRUCTURE

- **Turning on the Basic Infrastructure to Homes (Wiring, water and heat)**
For community members, the first signs to putting lives back together are the return of electricity and potable water. This will require many contractors and a structure plan to address neighborhoods – or grids – one at a time since these utilities require that each home/property must be occupied or monitored to avoid additional damage.

CITIZEN NEEDS

- **Throwing away too much –**
  Everyone should be cautious, but not too cautious. There must be clear guidelines pertaining to what personal items can be salvaged and cleaned and what needs to be thrown away due to personal/public health concerns. There may be an initial sense to throw away everything that got wet. That may not be the case and valuable items may be discarded needlessly.
- **Addressing Diversity** – Is everyone being treated equally?
- **Make recovery programs fit the needs of the people. Don't manipulate needs to fit programs.**
  Leaders and decision makers should continually listen to the public and to the on-site service providers about what needs are and are not being addressed with the available programs. Gaps in service must be recognized and then programs adjusted accordingly (which may require documented waivers "higher up").
- **Public input is essential - but not public control. Leaders will have to make hard choices.**
- **Reestablish sense of safety and neighborhood**
  Without a sense of security, residents will not be able to invest emotionally or financially in the recovery efforts. Businesses and industry will also not be able to reinvest.

  In addition to basic housing, citizens must also recover the sense of neighborhood and community – even in transitional or temporary housing units. Government should give them an opportunity to be part of a new neighborhood and they'll bring that sense of community back to old one (see below).

PSYCHOLOGICAL/MENTAL EFFECTS

- **Significance to mental health of getting people into homes and into neighborhoods.**
  Rebuilding the emotional/psychological infrastructure is equally as important as the physical infrastructure. Safety, belonging, and trust are the unseen bonds that will be necessary for long-term recovery. Grand Forks' transitional housing "FEMAville" was made up of travel trailers but local government added community by converting a nearby building into a day care and Community Recreation Center as well as produced a weekly neighborhood newsletter and other efforts such as a holiday-themed decorating contest for the trailers.
- **Psychological Stages of Recovery**
  - Denial
  - Anger
  - Bargaining
  - Depression
  - Acceptance
- **Re-establishing sense of protection – A requirement for necessary reinvestment. (See above)**
- **There will be a "New Normal" – not the same as before**
  Everyone will want to get back to how they were before the disaster but there will be many differences. Leaders should emphasize the there will be many differences and that these can/will be positive changes.
- **Long-range affects:**
  Mental Health issues are enormous after an event like this. Suicides or the "one car accident" increased after the flood. This was thought to be a way for the man-of-the-house to provide for his family via life insurance. Incidences of violence in the home increased, even violence among teenagers increased. In a 1998 United Way Needs Assessment Survey of Health & Human Service needs, the number one issue was Stress, Anxiety & Depression. In past surveys, this had always shown up, but never in the number one spot.

- **Robert Wood Johnson Foundation funded a population-based study of health conditions associated with the 1997 flooding in Grand Forks, North Dakota**
  - Researcher: Larry Burd, PhD;
  - Compared: Pre Flood Year: April 95 - March 97, Flood Year: April 97 - May 97, and Post Flood Year: June 97 - Jun 00
  - Data from the Hospital, Clinics, and 35 Community Agencies
- **Findings:**
  – Increase in Youth Truancy (schools)
  – Increases in Domestic Violence: 43%
  – Increase Driving Under Influence: 129%
  – Increase in Drug/Narcotic Violations: 275%
  – Increase in Mental Illness (Depression): 45%
  – Increase in Injuries: First 90 days
  – Increase in Respiratory (ages 20 - 64)
  – Increase in Infectious Disease
  – Increase in Nervous System Conditions
  – Population Decrease 3-4% (elderly)
- **Robert Wood Johnson Foundation funded a study of the impacts of the 1997 flood on health insurance in North Dakota**
  - Researcher: Alana Knudson-Buresh. PhD
  - Random telephone survey of 5,027 North Dakota Households from Feb 98 to May 98, with a response rate: 76.2%
- **Findings:**
  – Uninsured were the highest among people evacuated for two months or more
  – Uninsured were the highest as flood damage levels increased
  – Policy Implications:
   - Develop health insurance plans for displaced disaster victims
   - Provide access to health care professionals
   - Provide education about health insurance

Actions and Activities of the Regional Weather Information Center during the Historic Flood of 1997

Leon F. Osborne, Jr.

PRELUDE TO A FLOOD

The historic spring flood of 1997 had its genesis with heavy late summer and fall 1996 precipitation followed by a series of early and mid-winter heavy snowfalls. The late summer and fall precipitation elevated the water table across eastern North Dakota and northwestern Minnesota and provided with fall freeze-up: a barrier to immediate infiltration during the following spring snowmelt. The onset of winter storms also occurred earlier than normal with the first significant snowfall falling in the northeastern portion of the Red River Basin in mid-October and the first of twelve major winter storms affecting the western-most portions on October 26. This storm was accompanied by strong thunderstorms and tornadoes in Hubbard County of northwestern Minnesota. In mid-November, a major blizzard produced heavy snowfall across much of the region. Before the end of the winter, twelve major winter storms occurred across some portion of the Red River Basin. The National Weather Service (NWS) would end up classifying eight out of the twelve storms that impacted Grand Forks as blizzards.

The winter storms of the 1996-97 were exceptional, not only by the high numbers, but also from their source regions. While several of the lesser storms would frequently come from the northwest as Alberta Clippers, most the storms would come from either the west from Wyoming or from the southwest as Panhandle Hooks. In both latter situations, the storms moved into northeastern South Dakota where they slowed their forward speed for up to twelve to eighteen hours, thereby permitting deeper Gulf of Mexico moisture to move northward and become incorporated in the storm systems. This movement enhanced the eventual snowfall, particularly in the southern portion of the Red River Basin. Eventually, over the winter, snow totals would top eighty inches in the northern half of the Red River Basin and over one hundred inches in the south. The greatest amounts were found in LaMoure and Dickey Counties where as much as one hundred and twenty-five inches of snow fell.

These exceptional storms would prove to be a powerful test of a new advanced traveler weather information system (ATWIS) at the Regional Weather Information Center, housed at the University of North Dakota. The system was launched in the last week of October, in time for the first winter storm across the eastern part of North Dakota. The ATWIS was designed to provide en route traveler information on weather and road conditions across North Dakota and South Dakota interstate and US highways. It was an innovative experimental program that would prove valuable during the roadway flooding in North Dakota and South Dakota during the spring of 1997, despite extreme challenges during the Grand Forks flood. In future years, the success of this program would lead to it becoming the national model for the 511-traveler information system, still in use today.

A CONTROVERSIAL FLOOD PREDICTION

By the middle of January 1997, the snowfall continued to accumulate as strong winter storms and blizzards continued to rake the Northern Plains. By mid-January, Grand Forks had experienced five blizzards, along with periodic lesser snowstorms. A snow cover of over two feet was present, making a clear impression that this winter would likely lead to significant flooding of the rivers located in eastern North Dakota and northwestern Minnesota.

Local residents and politicians expressed concerns about possible impacts of spring flooding to ATWIS operations and others at the UND Regional Weather Information Center (RWIC). In particular, some worried about a possible disruption of telephone service at the Grand Forks AT&T facility.

To assess these impacts, the RWIC produced a simplified hydrologic model for the City of Grand Forks during the second half of January. The model evaluated the net water level of the Red River from an evaluation of water mass flux at a selected point south of the city compared to a corresponding point north. Using the existing base river flow levels at the time, along with estimated spring runoff of snowfall adding water to the upstream (south) point of the model, a predicted crest level was determined for the end of spring melt. We assumed that the rate of snow accumulation would continue as it already had for the winter, and that the snowmelt would occur in an optimum manner during March and early April. What was not included was any additional significant snowfall or heavy rain beyond the beginning of April. The results indicated a potential for a fifty-two-foot crest of the Red River. This not only suggested a record flood was possible, but also a possible threat to the operation of the ATWIS due to potential inundation of the streets around the Grand Forks AT&T facility.

Obviously, the results of the modeling created concerns for the sustainability of the ongoing RWIC research program; and while the efforts of performing the hydrologic modeling were for internal purposes and not meant for public knowledge, word soon leaked from RWIC to other university areas and beyond. Soon, RWIC was besieged with phone calls from curious individuals asking for details. When a news article written shortly thereafter called for a halt to the spread of flooding rumors, staff in RWIC did what they could to maintain a low-key profile and not be perceived as being a rumor mill. Unfortunately, the word was out about the RWIC flood prediction. Through the remainder of the winter and into the spring, discussion of a record-setting flood pervaded the region. While efforts were made to maintain a low public profile, the news of the RWIC flood prediction had generated a dialog with a variety of local government officials along with the North Dakota Congressional delegation. These discussions would continue and intensify as the spring snowmelt occurred and the assumptions of the model and the rise in the river levels were proving to be accurate.

CRAZY APRIL WEATHER AND THE FLOOD

By the end of March, it was obvious that major flooding would occur on the Red River. Efforts were underway across the entire Red River Basin to fight the rising waters. What was not anticipated was a wild early spring storm that would bring a combination of heavy rain, freezing rain, and a blizzard of major proportions. On the morning of April 4, 1997, a broad surface low pressure system was forming in the central portions of the US ahead of an upper-level trough and closed low over the southwestern US. This Panhandle Hook storm was ushering northward a deep layer of moist air from the Gulf of Mexico. A deep layer of Arctic air was poised to rush southward across North Dakota and western Canada and into central Montana. These ingredients led to strong rain bands forming across eastern North Dakota resulting in heavy precipitation falling on already rising floodwaters. This would make the sandbagging efforts underway at many places along the Red River more challenging and miserable to conduct. By the next day, April 5, the storm had evolved into a major ice storm across most of the Red River Valley and by evening the storm had transformed into a major blizzard. Until later that next day, the Red River Valley experienced snow and strong winds, most exceeding 50 mph. Some anemometers had frozen due to the freezing rain and true winds speeds were not available. Surface pressure analyses suggested some winds in the northern Red River Basin has exceeded 70 mph. Given the twenty-four hour/seven days a week operations schedule at RWIC to support the ATWIS, staffing of the facility required that the day shifts stays in place as the night shifts and the next day's shift could not make it to campus. As power was lost across campus and most of the town, the staff was eventually left with watching from the second-floor windows of Odegard Hall the bright flashes of power transformers, as they would explode and light the night sky through the howling blowing snow.

For many in the facility during the storm, it would be close to forty-hours before co-workers could relieve them. And while the greatest snowfall amounts of over two-feet were in southwestern North Dakota, the snow cover that had been melted prior to April 4 was now back to over one-half foot by April 7.

While the impact of the April 5-6 blizzard (commonly known as Hannah) on the final crest of the Red River in Grand Forks may never be fully known, it is certain that the blizzard increased concerns about a record flood and upped the urgency of flood fighting efforts. The efforts of the Regional Weather Information Center in flood fighting support became expanded almost immediately after the storm. Using the RWIC interface to Grand Forks' cable television network, around-the-clock support was provided on the latest weather and river information along with providing public service announcements on sandbagging efforts and the need for people to support the effort. This continuous support of the flood-fighting effort would continue until the midnight of April 18, when access to the cable system was lost. Staffing of RWIC had expanded to include many student volunteers who were willing to work long hours beyond their classes to assist with information delivery.

Many would work in addition to spending hours sandbagging at various areas throughout the city. The National Oceanic and Atmospheric Administration's (NOAA) River Forecast Center in Chanhassen, Minnesota provided assistance and information on ice jams. These ice jam observations were made initially by flight instructors in the UND Aviation Department and later by specific flights authorized by the Dean of Aerospace Sciences, John Odegard, to support the flood fighting efforts. RWIC served as the coordination center for the Odegard School's flood fighting efforts. In addition, work would continue with the ND Congressional Delegation on flooding events as RWIC staff was observing them while they were either engaged in sandbagging activities or conducting special fact-finding efforts for the delegation.

By April 17, many of the students working in RWIC had left campus. The uncertainty of the future and the rapid chain of events left many of the students in tears and in shock from what was occurring. Of course, the students were not the only ones struggling.

Some of RWIC's staff had already seen their homes or apartments succumb to the floodwaters — some losing all their possessions while they worked at RWIC to help others. With the evacuation order for much of the City of Grand Forks, this left RWIC with a serious challenge of staffing the ATWIS. This latter issue was of great concern because program leaders at the North Dakota and South Dakota Departments of Transportation and Federal Highway Administration decided that the ATWIS program would be canceled should the UND operations be halted for any reason. The conclusion that the ATWIS was an essential assistance for regions with flooded roads in North and South Dakota, as well as the rest of the regions of these states, put great pressure on the staff of RWIC to find a way to keep the program running.

However, a major turn for the worse occurred early on the morning of April 19. After the announcement of mandatory evacuation of Grand Forks, east of Washington Street, the number of available RWIC staff available was being rapidly depleted. Indeed, my family home was covered in this evacuation. While at Red River High School working to process my family's evacuation to the Grand Forks Air Force Base, I instead decided to evacuate my family to RWIC to keep the ATWIS running. So, my wife, three sons and the family dog relocated to RWIC early on April 19. By then, the skeleton staff remaining at RWIC were preparing to evacuate as well, leaving myself and one computer staff member to manage the ATWIS system going forward. Fortunately for the computer staff member, he lived west of Interstate 29 and could commute to work, even though security was tightened on campus; at times it became dicey for him to make it to RWIC.

Thus, from April 19 to April 28, the ATWIS and RWIC was operated by two individuals, one meteorologist and one computer scientist on an around-the-clock schedule until we were finally relieved by a meteorology staff member. My family assisted with managing the phones until my wife's place of employment reopened for business in Larimore on April 22. And while all water and air handling were off in Odegard Hall, before evacuating, John Odegard and Thomas Clifford made sure plenty of drinking water and food supplies were available to sustain us for weeks.

By the day the river crested on April 21, our practice of making road weather forecasts available every three hours for the ATWIS, checking water levels in the access tunnels of Odegard Hall, and fielding phone calls had become routine. However, some events were beyond routine: events such as an unwanted NBC national correspondent refusing to leave without a predetermined sound bite or the unannounced changing of the locks on Odegard Hall while staff was temporarily outside the building.

Since the RWIC had been active in providing flood-related information for much of the spring and aggressively in April, many individuals who had evacuated recognized RWIC as an information source and sought updates via telephone. These calls would occur any time of the day and often would be emotionally charged – seeking any possible information on their homes and the prospects for returning home. Fortunately, by attending daily briefings at UND Facilities where the Grand Forks Emergency Operations Center had been relocated after the basement of the Grand Forks Police Department flooded, I could be reasonably aware of the situation on the evolving flooding conditions. Because we're not able to provide information on individual houses, many calls were stressful experiences. We simply could not address the emotional concerns of the callers. This confusion also contributed to my own exasperation about not knowing the status of my own house.

After being joined by another RWIC staff meteorologist on April 28, I finally could return to my home to start my personal recovery. What I found was more fortunate than most; only my basement had flooded, and mostly with clean water. Within another week, more RWIC staff became available and together we successfully saved the ATWIS.

SUMMARY AND REFLECTION

From a meteorological perspective, the flood of 1997 was defined by a chain of events starting in the summer of 1996 and driven by a series of winter storms that, while not unprecedented in their occurrence, were statistically rare. And while such a chain of events is difficult, if not impossible, to predict, the accumulation of their results provides reasonable information to estimate future impacts on flooding potential. In that respect, the flood of 1997 provided lessons about predicting floods from winter snowmelt levels and how to prepare for extreme flooding events that continue to interest meteorological scientists to this day. From my personal perspective, the flood of 1997 was a professional challenge about whether, and to what extent, to provide flooding information to the public as a non-official source. I teach my students to understand the societal importance of what they do and how they can best benefit society. To this end, I still question what more could have been done by the RWIC and myself to benefit the local community during the flood of 1997.

Perhaps we could have done more to raise awareness of the potential magnitude of the flooding, or maybe the need to more strongly encourage people to press for flood insurance from agents who themselves were in denial of the potential severity of the flooding. In the end, it is amazing to look back at the flooding climax and recognize that it was history in the making and to know that what seemed like it occurred over weeks was only a few days at its peak of activity.

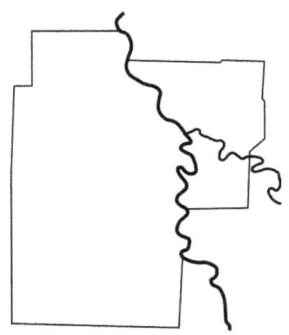

Studying Women in the Grand Forks Flood: A Sociologist Looks Back Twenty Years Later

Alice Fothergill

In April 1997, when Grand Forks was experiencing its historic flood, I was a sociology graduate student at the University of Colorado. National news had been covering the devastation of the Red River Flood and the dramatic downtown fire; at the Hazards Research Center in Boulder where I worked, we had all been watching closely. I had been planning my dissertation project on women and disaster, and so it was not a huge surprise when my dissertation advisor summoned me to his office and gave me the news: I was headed to Grand Forks.

I arrived in Grand Forks on a warm afternoon the first week of June. The city was in the midst of cleaning and rebuilding. Disasters have long been considered unique laboratories and strategic sites to learn about social life as they reveal social conditions usually hidden; at the same time, disasters are social – not "natural" – phenomenon and have their foundation in the social structure. Thus, Grand Forks was chosen to become a research setting to study women's experiences. I had never been to Grand Forks, did not know anyone, and did not know what to expect. It turned out to have been the perfect town for my study and an important first step in my career as a disaster sociologist.

In Grand Forks, I was a true "outsider" when I conducted my research. This had its advantages and disadvantages. Since I arrived with little background knowledge of North Dakota in general, and Grand Forks and East Grand Forks in particular, I had a lot to learn. As I slowly made my way around town, establishing contacts, and recruiting participants for interviews, the residents of Grand Forks welcomed me. They patiently explained what their terms meant, where things were located, how the city worked, and who was who. Residents, including several UND faculty members, provided assistance such as housing, background information, and support. Because I was an outsider, people realized I needed the full story, with background and details. In many ways, it was an advantage as I tried to understand life before and after the flood. I remember long extended conversations with residents; I recall sitting at picnic tables next to gutted homes. These people were sad and exhausted, but gave me their time; I still feel honored and grateful for their generosity.

One thing I learned in my interviews with the survivors of the Grand Forks flood was that they wanted to help others, even in the midst of their own recovery needs. Despite differences in backgrounds, the women I interviewed shared this desire to contribute to preparedness efforts and the recovery of others. Like other residents, they spent hours sandbagging before the flood and helped family and friends move items to high ground. Afterwards, in the midst of the destruction, they listened to each other at kitchen tables; they helped scrub flood-soaked belongings; they comforted family and friends; they helped drag destroyed belongings to the curb. Indeed, I believe that is why some of the women volunteered to be part of my study—they wanted to assist me and were concerned that not enough participants would volunteer.

At the same time, however, the women struggled with accepting assistance themselves in the disaster aftermath. They felt stigmatized and humiliated to receive assistance of any kind in a culture that stresses self-sufficiency, independence, privacy, and adheres to the norm of reciprocity. Their view of a welfare recipient was of someone who does not work hard or takes advantage of the system. Some of the Grand Forks women tried to manage this stigma of charity by writing thank you notes and showing others, including me, photos of their former homes. For many, confronting these feelings of embarrassment and shame made them realize that they held certain beliefs about poverty and welfare, and through their own experience with the flood, their ideology began to shift and they developed new empathy for the poor. They realized that others who receive assistance around the country are also going through a crisis – not a flood, perhaps, but maybe the loss of a job, or an illness –and they, too, are deserving of assistance.

The women of Grand Forks made a valuable contribution to an emerging field of study in 1997, at a time when social scientists knew very little about women's experiences in disasters. By sharing their detailed stories and experiences, that knowledge gap began to be filled. Disaster sociologists learned from them the ways in which their labor contributed to the recovery of their families and communities. We understand more about how gendered expectations led them to take on the majority of caregiving responsibilities, of children and elderly family members. From their stories, we learned about rapid downward mobility after disasters and the difficulties of navigating the post-disaster bureaucracy. Their honesty helped us to see how women cope with domestic violence in disasters. These women's experiences taught us that recovery is long, and one's social class, age, and ability status can shape that recovery. They also helped illustrate how recreating their domestic culture and reestablishing rituals, such as holiday meals, helped them and their families recover. My research on the women of Grand Forks was at the beginning of an avalanche of research on gender and disaster in the years that followed. Thankfully, disaster sociologists are still hard at work filling this knowledge gap.

Over the years, I stayed in touch with many of the women in the study. We exchanged holiday cards, baby shower invitations, change of address announcements, and wedding photos. Sometimes they simply sent notes with updates on their lives: "I am writing to tell you that I'm getting a divorce;" "Our daughter is still sick from the chemicals from the rebuilding materials;" "This year is the first year since the flood that things feel sort of 'normal';" "The river is flooding again." The notes were a reminder that a disaster can have myriad and complicated effects. I traveled to Grand Forks six times in 1997 and 1998, and it was a pleasure getting to know the women and sometimes their families. As I wrote my book on the study's findings, I wanted to make sure that it truly reflected, as much as possible, their experiences. I felt like I owed them that much.

Eight years after the flood, in 2005, I had the opportunity to return to Grand Forks. My goal was to visit with as many women in the study as possible, personally deliver a copy of the book, and thank them in person. The UND Bookstore held a book-signing event for me and several of the study participants attended. I was also able to see many women in their new or redone homes, which was particularly meaningful. I vividly remember walking through Lincoln Drive Park with one woman who had lost her home in that neighborhood. We walked until we found the spot where her home once stood; she recognized the trees in her former yard. We stood there together and she was overcome with emotion. It still signified an overwhelming loss for her. She, like other women in the study, had shown us the significance of losing a home and one's belongings; how identity and sense of self can be intimately tied to home. While it is rare for disaster researchers to return to disaster sites they have studied, I found that visit to be one of the most valuable and moving moments of my research career.

Over the years since then, I have followed Grand Forks in the news, crossing my fingers when I hear about high levels in the Red River, and thinking of all those who I had the privilege of interviewing. I live in New England now and do research on other disasters, but Grand Forks holds a special place for me. I am still immensely grateful for all that I learned there, the women who shared their stories, and all the generosity shown me during one of the most challenging moments in the town's history.

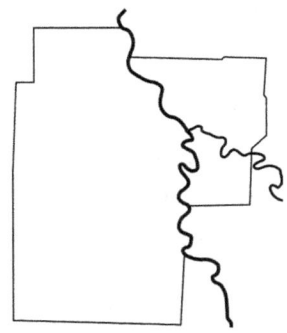

A Conversation with Eliot Glassheim

The Need for Self-Expression

David Haeselin

Eliot Glassheim remembers. In fact, one could argue that Glassheim's work is the single most valuable resource for helping us remember the 1997 in the ways that we do. Glassheim's oral history – *Voices from the Flood* – and his book-length examination of the decision-making processes during the initial recovery – *Behind the Scenes* – stand as some of the most humane and cogent responses to the disaster. Ask him about these books and Glassheim is quick to tell you that he didn't do it alone. Laurel Reuter of the North Dakota Museum of Art organized the production of the book, supervised its publication, and much more. Professor Kim Porter of the UND Department of History wrote the volume *Ordinary Heroes* and compiled material for the books. Glassheim conducted only some of the interviews in the book, but he did edit them into the book as it now stands. All this reminds us that one can't write a good history without listening to the voices of others.

Glassheim and I met at Urban Stampede Coffee House in downtown Grand Forks, a historic building that, like so many of the important places in Grand Forks, somehow managed to survive the flood, fire, and urban development during the two decades of recovery. When I asked Glassheim about what he was most proud of in relation to the flood, he answered in his characteristic self-deprecating way. "I love to bullshit," he told me. This wasn't exactly an answer, but I think he replied in this way because of the way he refuses to take credit for the work of other people. Our two-hour conversation, however, did add credence to his response; there's no doubt that the man has the gift of gab.

"I don't really think recovery is on anyone's mind anymore," Glassheim told me early in our conversation. Indeed, everyone I've talked to who lived through the flood considers Grand Forks' recovery a remarkable success. This success is in great part thanks to the work of Glassheim, the city council, and the local politicians and decision makers who steered the city in the months after the flood. Above all, Glassheim attributes this accomplishment to the citizens of Grand Forks and the remarkable investment of time and money from state and federal governmental agencies.

There's no denying that Grand Forks got lucky in terms of the scope of federal assistance. But this inflow of attention and funding raised the stakes for many of the decisions that Glassheim and his cohort needed to make. The sheer volume of decisions necessary to get the city running again and get it back to some sort of normalcy is staggering still. Especially in the wake of an unprecedented disaster, decisions needed to be made, and they needed to be made quickly.

"I'm pretty laid back, but the flood changed my outlook," Glassheim told me. He then shared a story to illustrate this point. His conversion came during a city council meeting where he and his compatriots were debating the cost of a plumber's license. This may seem an asinine topic, but the councilors were worried about an influx of unlicensed plumbers who might take advantage of unsuspecting flood victims. Their conversation dragged on for around forty minutes. This would be fine during a normal, sparsely attended city council meeting, but this was no ordinary meeting—hundreds were in attendance. The people of Grand Forks were worried and angry, and the city council was spending the better part of an hour debating a minor point. Eventually, an attendee stood up, interrupted the councilors and asked: "What about our homes?" Glassheim took the not-so subtle hint and urged others to do so as well. After the meeting, he helped draft eight motions that were put into effect like machine-gun fire at the beginning of the next meeting. "Bam, bam, bam, bam." That's how the next meeting started. Glassheim understood things differently now. From then on "I was big on getting things done," he said.

Glassheim learned through this experience that decision makers should do just that: decide. He felt that people wanted their local government to act and not wring their hands so much. In this, he feels that the council took their constituents into account by making swift, confident decisions. "They made their voices heard. We had a mission. We had marching orders," Glassheim summarized. This sense of decisive action seems counter to the prevailing worldview of a writer and editor like Glassheim. He described this shift in his own outlook as correctly sensing the changing zeitgeist of the town. He was the only member who wasn't thrown off the council in the election following the flood. More, Mayor Pat Owens also lost her spot. "People were angry. People wanted change," Glassheim noted.

This observation turned our conversation to the current political climate of the United States in early 2017. Whichever side of the aisle you sit on, it's safe to say that political discourse is divisive. As tragic and painful as the flood was, one positive aspect of it was forcing people come together, to rally around the common mission of rebuilding. In the wake of a disaster, "people are going to start talking to each other," he said. Along those lines, I think we can understand Glassheim's flood books as a continuation of this imperative. The victims the flood used one of the oldest human inventions to process their communal pain. These people told each other stories to help get through it.

When I asked about how he thinks his work stands the test of time, Glassheim turned shy. This seemed strange for a man known for his sense of humor and relish at chewing the fat. "I don't have a very rich emotional register," he told me, but even after just knowing him for a couple of hours, I find that hard to believe. Glassheim and the others responsible for the NDMoA books took it upon themselves to give the people of the Red River Valley a venue for their voices, a chance to document their losses and the way they made it through. Looking back on the process, Glassheim noted the depression, even ennui, that struck so many survivors.

These people had emotional attachments to things that were lost forever. "Your identity is tied up in those things," he observed. This observation is only more relevant now. Memories have been invested elsewhere into new things and new places, but what stories do they tell?

I would define identity as the stories we tell about who we think we are. Some of this is about where we come from, and thus, the photographs that were lost forever weaken the survivors' sense of the past. Identity is also about what we do — our jobs, our hobbies, our family lives. Even though no one lost their lives during the flood of 1997, many people had to process great shocks to who they were. And if they couldn't rebound completely from that, can they really be called the same people?

Looking back on our conversation now, something jumps out at me. Throughout our freewheeling chat, Glassheim barely mentioned his own losses. Sure, he is lucky enough to still live in same house of North Third street as he did before the flood, but there's something more to it. Glassheim had something to focus on above and beyond his personal turmoil. His identity was already structured around the community via his role as a politician, and the flood forced him concentrate on telling that version of the story and eliciting similar ones from others.

Not everyone's identity managed to recover in the ways that Grand Forks itself did. But the documentary work of Glassheim and the NDMoA should be remembered for their role in protecting the identity of Grand Forks that remains strong today. "There was a need for self-expression," Glassheim remembered. And he and the rest of the team gave people that chance. It only makes sense that if your voice isn't heard you stop speaking up. While describing his editorial method, Glassheim noted that he self-consciously tried to talk with and edit the voices of a representative group of people including those with whom he didn't see eye-to-eye, even some people he didn't particularly like.

But that's what citizenship is about — working with others to get shit done. Glassheim explained his work as a part of the larger human project, and one germane to the project of the humanities. He described his oral history as attempting to "educate people for citizenship, and seeing both sides of the issue; for being part of a discussion." As we were leaving the coffee shop, Glassheim asked me to tell him about the goals of the book you are now reading. I explained it as an experience of learning about others — for my students, for people new to Grand Forks, for readers coping with their own recoveries from other natural and emotional disasters, for myself. I tried to make the case that there are intellectual benefits to feeling like an outsider. It makes you into a listener, a noticer. In delving into the material history of the flood, I hoped to give my students and readers a way to better understand the range of emotional and social responses to catastrophe. Glassheim listened closely to my spoken version of this answer, waited for me to finish, considered it for a moment, and then replied: "I think that you are doing important work."

It shouldn't take a disaster to get us talking to one another, but we must remember how the flood fostered a sense of camaraderie and unity. Indeed, other voices included in this collection have lamented how quickly these feelings waned. When things started to get back to normal, people felt the overwhelming need to protect what was theirs: to fight for a fair buyout if their home had to be bulldozed, to get as much recovery money as they could to ensure the physical and mental health of their family. Even a fleeting moment of communal purpose offers one clear instance of a time when the public good outweighed the personal. Floods wash away memories, but I hope that this collection will help others remember the possibility of self-expression that exceeds selfish needs.

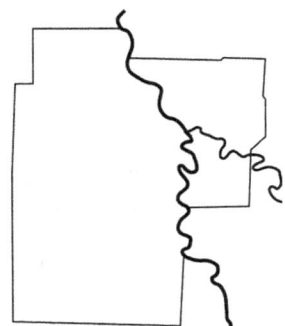

The '97 Flood: Epic or Episode?

Mike Jacobs

The Flood of 1997 was a major event in Grand Forks, certainly ranking historically with the arrival of the railroad, the founding of the University and the location of the Air Force Base. It's been called "epic," but that may be because we humans like hyperbole. Or it may be that we like to go biblical.

The flood and its aftermath did reshape Grand Forks physically, moving structures away from the river and establishing broad swathes of parkland and open space. These are permanent changes, at least as long as the flood is remembered. The flood had an impact on the city's sense of itself and on its political culture, as well. Grand Forks institutions were profoundly changed. Twenty years on, it is too soon to assess whether these changes will endure.

Winter came early in 1996, the year before the flood. The first blizzard, named Andy by the *Grand Forks Herald*, struck on Nov. 16. Early the next morning, Francis Delabreau, a UND student disappeared after a party. A season-long and citywide search was undertaken. His body was found on Feb. 2. The disappearance and desperate search added to the sense of foreboding, as storm after storm dumped more and more snow, about 100 inches in all.

The last blizzard was the worst. "Hard-hearted Hannah" struck on the first weekend in April, bringing rain, sleet and ice ahead of another foot of snow. Powerlines were snapped and poles downed.

Thousands were left in the dark, including a large share of Grand Forks' population. Hannah ended sandbagging operations that were under way along the river. The storm was followed almost immediately by rapid warming and rising rivers through the Red River basin. The eventual impact was catastrophic, the worst flood in the city's history. Without Hannah, this story probably would have been different; the flood might have been held back.

As the snow fell that winter, Grand Forks was a small city built close to a small river near the nation's northern border. A system of dikes provided protection to a river level of 49 feet, the previous record river crest. That crest had occurred less than twenty years previously, in 1979, and Grand Forks beat that flood. There was frantic sandbagging, but the dikes held. Residents on the west side of town weren't so lucky. A surge from the English Coulee, a 30-mile long tributary of the Red River, flooded some homes. Still, the '79 flood left Grand Forks confident that it could meet whatever threat the river presented.

Despite the foreboding as the winter of '97 drew on, a sense of confidence remained. Preparations began in February. Citizens gathered at Sandbag Central to prepare. Emergency operations were planned. Neighborhood flood watch groups were organized. Normalcy prevailed. A downtown café hosted a drag show called "Blood Red River," in which a different local celebrity played the part of a murder victim every Saturday night. That is, until the week of April 19. That killer was never identified; the flood intervened.

Before the flood, downtown was funky. An antique mall filled several storefronts inside the downtown shopping center. There was a candy store and a kiosk offering Norwegian cuisine, including klub and krumkakke. Across the street, a small shop sold kitsch items from the 1950s and 1960s. It was a downtown aspiring to be something. There was a drugstore with a pharmacy. The city's largest bank occupied a prominent corner, as did the newspaper.

Neighborhoods called Riverside, Central Park and Lincoln Drive were built close to the river. Mostly these were areas of modest houses – though each of the areas had at least a few stately turn-of-the-century homes. Farther south, along Reeves Drive,

Belmont Road and Elmwood, houses were bigger and costlier. The river invaded them all.

Flood forecasters had predicted a crest at 49 feet, a level that Grand Forks had beaten only 18 years before. The National Weather Service stuck to a prediction at 49 feet. But the river rose higher, cresting at 54.1 feet on April 19th. An angry homeowner just east of the Kennedy Bridge painted on his ruined house, "49 Feet? My Ass!"

The flood transformed Grand Forks immediately. National media descended, and Grand Forks saw itself depicted as a heroic community that could meet the crisis. Help of many kinds arrived, from private charities such as the Red Cross and Salvation Army, individuals arriving with mops and hammers, and even consumer goods: from T-shirts to grapefruit juice to canned water from Anheuser Busch. Big money came from McDonald's heiress Joan Kroc, James Lee Witt, director of the Federal Emergency Management Agency, and Andrew Cuomo, secretary of the Housing and Urban Development Department. The state sent the National Guard. Governor Ed Schafer and members of Congress came. There was a tremendous sense of challenge and achievement, and an understanding that people cared and the government could get it right. There were hugs and high hopes. On the day the river crested, President Bill Clinton himself arrived with a message of hope. "It's okay to be brokenhearted," he told the community.

City leaders radiated optimism. The mayor was Pat Owens, a career clerk in City Hall who'd moved into the mayor's office less than a year before. She presided over a city council of fourteen members, two selected from each of seven wards. She immediately appointed a committee of business leaders to help plan the city's recovery, and she established something she called "the tri-chairs" to manage city operations.

An era of good feeling prevailed.

In this interim, voters approved building an events center, now the Alerus Center, for concerts, athletic events and conventions, now affectionately called "The Al." Ralph Engelstad announced his gift of $100 million to build the nation's finest college hockey venue. It didn't take long to dub this monument "The Ralph."

Later a fitness center, funded by private donors, was built on the south end of town.

But the good feeling didn't last.

The mayor's government structure proved clumsy, even unworkable. Frustration with city bureaucracy grew. There was protracted controversy about dike lines, for example, and bad feeling about how both public and private aid was spent. Owens had rallied the city and inspired the nation, but she lost her bid for reelection just three years after the flood. Mike Brown, a physician from the south end of town, was motivated to run because of delays in decisions about future flood control in his neighborhood.

The political structure of the city changed. In time, so did the political personalities. Elected in 2000, Brown has survived three elections to preside at the twentieth anniversary observation. All seven members are new to the city council. Three are new to the city since the flood. Of the others, one was one of the tri-chairs; the others are new to city government.

New community projects have encountered opposition. A drive to build a new library– replacing a structure form the 1970s – suffered a setback when voters rejected a sales tax to pay for it 2011. The project seems stalled. Voters dealt another blow that November when they rejected a sales tax that would have built a fund for infrastructure projects ranging from water treatment to roads and potentially an interstate highway interchange. It was presented as preparing the city for the next three decades.

Members of the community offered new expansive proposals: for a children's museum, and for an arts venue, including a much larger North Dakota Museum of Art. There was talk of "vibrancy zones" of new, hip restaurants and retail shops, and even of a public transportation system with dedicated routes, a kind of bus-rail. A "public arts" initiative was undertaken. Forty-Second Street was to become an arts corridor linking the UND campus, The Al and the shopping mall.

There's talk still, and even some anticipation.

All of this feels like old times. The event center was passed on its third try; it took two elections to build Columbia Road Overpass and a third to widen it to four lanes. The rejection of the library and the infrastructure tax recalled an old political culture, a culture of skepticism and animosity toward city government and its leadership.

The city faces other challenges. Downtown has changed. The largest bank moved much of its operation out of downtown, though its headquarters remain. The newspaper built its production facility west of the interstate highway and out of harm's way, though its newsroom and business operations remain downtown. A popular bakery boasting local ingredients closed and sits empty.

There is new controversy.

After the flood, a vacant city lot was turned into something called "Arbor Park." A proposal to develop the lot prompted a petition drive demanding a public vote.

The park is reminiscent of that funkiness that prevailed downtown before the flood. It's next door to an art gallery and a creative art studio. There's a local coffee shop on the corner and just past that another pocket park, a pizza joint with rooftop seating and another art gallery. Around the next corner, there's another pocket park. Elsewhere downtown, there's new housing, both apartments and condominiums. Space that the city made available for shops and offices has gradually filled up. It's just starting to seem vibrant.

Across the river, East Grand Forks' story has been different. Its flood mayor, Lynn Stauss, remained in office until 2016. A major sporting goods store filled up much of the space that the flood cleared out; a mall with a 15-plex movie theater took more of it. There's a restaurant row facing the riverfront. East Grand Forks has become the entertainment destination in the community.

One part of this exploded into public controversy. The city failed to recover its loan for one of the restaurants, owned by the mayor's brother. This reflected the city's past. "The Eastside" has a more free-wheeling heritage, dating at least to the days when Minnesota was wet and North Dakota was dry. The city has had a succession of confident, even colorful mayors, and the office is more powerful than its counterpart west of the river. Like Grand Forks, though, East Grand Forks has reverted to the pre-flood political culture.

It is too early to know, twenty years later, if the Flood of '97 will continue to have a transformative impact on Grand Forks, as the railroad, the University and the Air Force Base have had. Right now, it seems that the old town is back – built bigger and better, facing new challenges, but still stuck to its earlier political culture: a culture of criticism and caution, not one of innovation and risk. This is perhaps because Grand Forks has always played above its rank, and voters have pulled back their dreams to a more realistic level.

A preliminary conclusion, twenty years after the flood, was an episode in the city's history, not an epic event. The flood brought change, certainly, but it didn't change everything.

911 Call

Offer Our Home

April 18, 1997, 8:48 p.m.
Call 1802
Abstract by Matthew Nelson; quality assurance by Matthew Nelson.

Audio Link: https://perma.cc/D3V3-WJEU

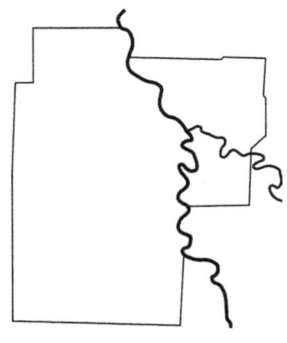

Incoming on channel 24, April 18, 1997, 8:48 p.m.

Dispatcher: Law enforcement center.
Caller: Yes, I'm not sure if I'm calling the right number, but we haven't heard a number for a long time to offer our home for people in need. Do you happen to know what number we can call?
Dispatcher: For what?
Caller: To offer our home to a shelter for people who have to evacuate.
Dispatcher: I would call down to EOC. 7-4-6-2-6-8-5. If you just called that number, you probably just got us because you they are getting such a high volume of calls down there now because of the evacuation. So I would just keep trying as much as I can. Okay?
Caller: Okay, thanks!
Dispatcher: You're welcome! Bye!

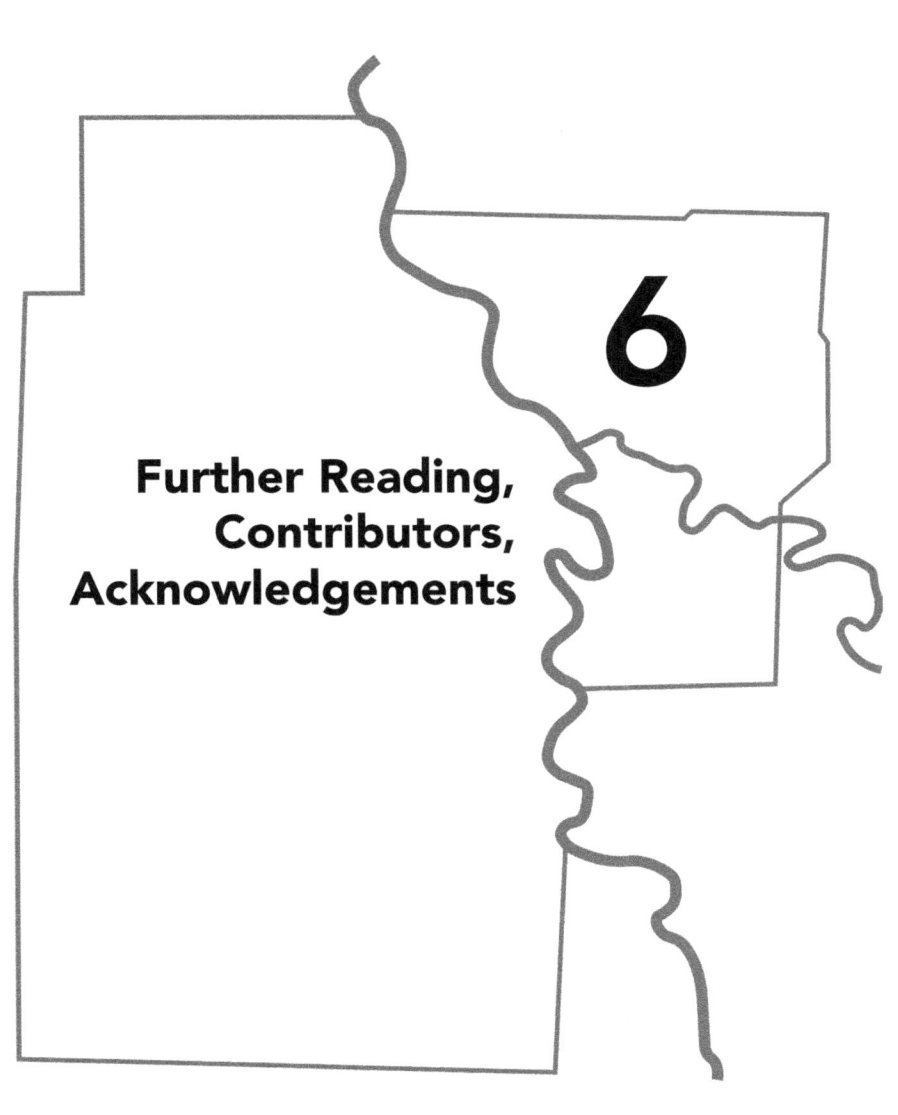

Further Reading, Contributors, Acknowledgements

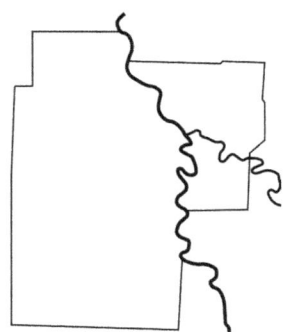

Suggestions for Further Reading

EDITED COLLECTIONS

Glassheim, Eliot, Kimberly K. Porter and Robin Silverman (eds). *Behind the Scenes*. Grand Forks: North Dakota Museum of Art, 2002.

Glassheim, Eliot (ed). *Voices from the Flood: An Oral History of the 1997 Flood of the Red River of the North*. Grand Forks: North Dakota Museum of Art, 1999.

Hylden, Eric and Laurel Reuter (eds.). *Under the Whelming Tide*. Grand Forks: North Dakota Museum of Art, 1998.

Jacobs, Mike (ed). *Come Hell and High Water: The Incredible Story of the 1997 Red River Flood*. Grand Forks: Grand Forks Herald and Knight-Ridder Newspapers, 1997.

Orvik, Jan and Dick Larson. *The Return of Lake Agassiz: The University of North Dakota and the Flood of 1997*. Grand Forks: The University of North Dakota, 1998.

Quam, Jennifer. *A Small Town's War: East Grand Forks 1997 Flood Fight*. East Grand Forks: City of East Grand Forks, 1999.

Sprung, Christopher (ed.) *Fighting Back: The Blizzards and Floods in the Red River Valley, 1996-97*. Fargo: Forum Communications Company, 1997.

SINGLE AUTHOR BOOKS

Fothergill, Alice. *Heads Above Water: Gender, Class, and Family in the Grand Forks Flood*. Albany: State University of New York Press, 2004.

Porter, Kim. *Uncommon Heroes: The City of Grand Forks Flood Fight, 1997*. Grand Forks: North Dakota Museum of Art, 1998.

Shelby, Ashley. *Red River Rising: The Anatomy of a Flood and the Survival of an American City*. St. Paul: Borealis Books, 2003.

Varley, Jane. *Flood Stage and Rising*. Lincoln: University of Nebraska Press, 2005.

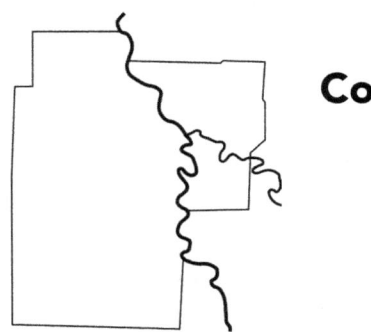

Contributors

David Haeselin, PhD, is an instructor in the English department at the University of North Dakota, where he teaches courses in the Writing, Editing, and Publishing certificate program. Broadly, Dr. Haeselin is interested in finding ways to better explain the work of the humanities and the sciences to the public. To that end, his work with the Digital Press @ UND, the WEP program, and other collaborative ventures on campus all attempt to bring academic knowledge directly to the publics it often speaks for and about. His recent writing appears in *Critique: Studies in Contemporary Fiction*, *Hybrid Pedagogy*, *The Los Angeles Review of Books*, and *Codex*, an art book written by Micah Bloom, due out from the DP@UND in Fall 2017.

Michael Brown, M.D, is the 26th and current Mayor of Grand Forks, North Dakota. He was elected in 2000, the first election after the flood, and has served as Mayor ever since. He was appointed to Federal Emergency Management Agency board in 2007. Dr. Brown is an obstetrician in the Altru Health System in Grand Forks.

Alice Fothergill is an Associate Professor of Sociology at the University of Vermont. In 2017, she was a Fulbright Fellow in New

Zealand studying children and disaster. Her award-winning book, *Children of Katrina* (2015, University of Texas Press), written with Lori Peek, examines the experiences of children and youth in the aftermath of Hurricane Katrina. Professor Fothergill, a native of Washington, D.C., is an editor of *Social Vulnerability to Disasters* (2010, 2013, Taylor & Francis), first and second editions. In the aftermath of Tropical Storm Irene in Vermont in 2011, she created service-learning projects for her students to help with the recovery and she has conducted research and published several articles on volunteerism in the aftermath of the September 11, 2001 terrorist attacks in New York City. Her first book, *Heads Above Water: Gender, Class, and Family in the Grand Forks Flood* (2004, SUNY Press) examines women's experiences in the 1997 flood in Grand Forks, North Dakota. Professor Fothergill's areas of scholarship and teaching include family and childhood studies, disaster vulnerability, gender, inequality, service learning, and qualitative methods.

Eliot Glassheim grew up in New York City and moved to Grand Forks, North Dakota, "for one year" in 1971. He stayed and has been active in the political and cultural life of the city. He was a member of the Grand Forks City council for 30 years and a North Dakota State Representative for 22 years. He is the author of *Sweet Land of Decency* (a book of stories from American history), and three collections of poetry, *The Restless Giant*, *Foreign Exchange* (in collaboration with his wife, Dyan Rey, a regionally renowned painter), and *Passing Through*. He is at work on a fourth collection of poetry.

Leon F. Osborne, Jr. is a Chester Fritz Distinguished Professor of Atmospheric Sciences at the University of North Dakota. He is also Director or the UND Regional Weather Information Center, which is devoted to providing weather information to support academics and research on campus and to providing decision-support information to individuals and organizations across North Dakota and the surrounding States. In his almost thirty-nine years at UND he has conducted research and has been recognized by the Ford Foundation and the Harvard Kennedy School of Government for its innovation. Prof. Osborne is also a recipient of the National Governor's Association Award for Outstanding Service to State Government. Leon is a native of northwest Texas.

Gordon L. Iseminger has been teaching at the University of North Dakota since 1962, where he currently holds the rank of Chester Fritz Distinguished Professor of History. Professor Iseminger has written widely on a variety of historical subjects including the making of the North Dakota/South Dakota state line in his book *The Quartzite Border* (1988).

Mike Jacobs is editor emeritus at *The Grand Forks Herald*.

Lee Murdock is a retired physics and chemistry teacher. His prior writing experience was weighted heavily toward chemical reagent bottle labels for his lab but since his retirement, his writings have been published in anthologies, specialty sections of newspapers, *Dakota Country*, a regional Hunting and Fishing magazine and t*he Good Old Days* magazine. To keep from being forgotten, he has published a book of his memoirs and essays for his descendant, which is available on Amazon. His sense of humor is derived from growing up on a rural farm and 38 years of teaching. Both have provided him fodder for many of his personal memoirs and essays. He resides in North Dakota with his wife, June.

Sherry O'Donnell is a Professor of English at the University of North Dakota. She has published articles and given talks on animals in performance, the pet/livestock/wild game spectrum, and some classical origins of pastoral nostalgia. She lives on Beau Pre Farm in Minnesota, where she raises ancient-breed sheep for food, fiber, and breeding stock. She is a member of Minnesota Grown, a sustainable agriculture organization connecting farmers to consumers. Her free-range chickens supply eggs to Amazing Grains Food Co-op in Grand Forks. Professor O'Donnell and her partner Virgil Benoit hosted a family and their three dogs during the 1997 Flood. They stayed for six weeks, as did many flood refugees who found temporary homes among farm families along the Red and Red Lake Rivers.

Janet Rex is originally from Wisconsin, but she has lived in Grand Forks for many years. She has MA degrees in English (University of North Dakota) and Library Science (University of Wisconsin—Madison), she has BA degrees in Sociology/Anthropology and

Religion (Ripon College), and she is currently a reference librarian and Coordinator of Distance Education Services at the Chester Fritz Library, University of North Dakota.

Josh Roiland is an Assistant Professor and CLAS-Honors Preceptor of Journalism in the Department of Communication and Journalism and the Honors College at the University of Maine. He has a Ph.D. in American Studies from St. Louis University. He researches, writes, and teaches classes on the theory and practice of literary journalism, journalism and American democracy, and the nonfiction of David Foster Wallace. His writing has appeared in *the Washington Post*, *Longreads*, *Nieman Storyboard*, *A24 Films*, and *Literary Journalism Studies*. His most recent essay "A Shot in the Arm"—about academic debt—was published *on Longreads* in February 2017.

Lynn Stauss was the Mayor of East Grand Forks from 1995 until his retirement at the end of 2016.

Ken Vein is the Administrative Director, Plant and Facilities at Altru Health System. He also serves on the Grand Forks City Council, and was the lead engineer during the flood of 1997.

STUDENT EDITORS

Montana Anderson is English major at the University of North Dakota working on her Writing, Editing, and Publishing certificate. After graduation, she plans to move to an urban center and continue working with books in the publishing industry. When not working, she enjoys binge-watching Netflix and having an entire pizza all to herself.

Aly Baumer is a senior double-majoring in English and Secondary Education at the University of North Dakota. She hopes to move back to her hometown in Minnetonka, MN to pursue a teaching career after graduation. Aly currently focuses on a Middle School Minor and strives to instill a love of reading among middle school students. When she is not teaching, she loves to play soccer and go skiing.

Nik Chartrand is from Winnipeg, Canada and a senior English literature student at the University of North Dakota. She is also minoring in Communications and attaining a certificate in Editing and Writing. After graduating with her B.A in December 2017, Nik plans to attend graduate school for an M.S in Publishing. Nik is very passionate about books and hopes that with her degrees, she can increase world literacy.

Sheilan Hamasoor is an undergraduate student majoring in English and minoring in International Studies. She is also attaining a certificate in Editing and Publishing at the University of North Dakota. After graduation, she hopes to attend law school. Sheilan's love of literature started when she was first able to read, and that passion has continued throughout her life. Sheilan also has a passion for music and in her free time, she plays the violin in the chamber orchestra at UND and the Greater Grand Forks Symphony Orchestra.

Luke Jirik, from Prior Lake, MN, is an undergraduate at the University of North Dakota, pursuing a BA in English in addition to a certificate in Editing and Publishing. Luke also works as a research assistant for his department, as well as creates content for a social blogging platform – his love of reading, writing, and the English language started at the elementary age and continues to carry with him in both the professional and recreational spheres of his life. Luke hopes to move to the Minneapolis/St. Paul area after graduation and work in the editing/publishing industry in the area.

Ali Liffrig is an English major at the University of North Dakota, with a German minor and a Certificate in Writing and Editing. She comes from Minnesota and is academically interested in linguistics, literature, cultural differences, and international relations. Ali graduates in May and plans to seek employment in either the publishing industry or the international community. She enjoys trying out new recipes and playing with dogs in her free time.

Lloyd Norstedt is a senior English major at the University of North Dakota. Lloyd grew up in Harvey, North Dakota, but would like to live in Seattle someday. Lloyd loves animals, playing video games, and reading.

Hal Olson was born and raised in the Oslo and East Grand Forks, Minnesota. She graduated high school from East Grand Forks in 2014 and will be graduating from UND with a bachelor's degree in English and a minor in philosophy. She plans to pursue a PhD in English.

Michala Prigge is an English graduate with a minor in Women and Gender Studies. She realized her passion for writing after taking a few creative writing and English courses. English 334 was a creative way to become involved in the community she grew to love and her passion for writing and people expanded. She has presented her research at the Red River Women's Conference. After college, she plans to teach English in Thailand for a year and then decide whether she wants to continue as a teacher, or obtain her MFA in creative writing.

Brendon Saseangbong is originally from Honolulu, Hawaii and moved to Minnesota when he was very young. He is currently studying English at the University of North Dakota and hopes to pursue a career in technical writing or teaching. He has a strong interest in old literature and have favorites like Beowulf and The Epic of Gilgamesh. He plans to move back Hawaii or California after graduating. In his spare time, Brendon enjoys reading Japanese novels and listening to Korean musicians like Epik High.

Kristie Schmit is an English major at the University of North Dakota. She first became interested in editing and publishing during her senior year of high school in Kindred, North Dakota. She wanted to turn reading, something she enjoyed doing for years, into a career. After graduating in 2017, Kristie hopes to find a job at a small or independent press where she can put into practice all that the UND English program has taught her. When she is not busy, she spends her time baking or lounging on the couch with her dog.

Brian Walls is a Grand Forks resident and flood survivor, majoring in English at the University of North Dakota. Brian served four years active duty in the United States Marine Corps, and was honorably discharged as a Sergeant after two combat tours.

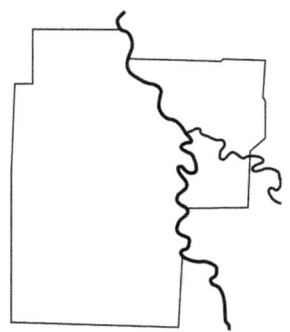

Acknowledgements

All books are the work of many, this book more than most. First, I need to express my debt of gratitude to the student editors. Without their tireless effort, keen creativity, and sharp eye for detail, there would be no book. I also need to thank the staff of the Elywn B. Robinson Department of Special Collections at the Chester Fritz Library: Curt Hanson, Michael Swanson, and Bret Baier. No request was ever too much; thank you for facilitating this new chapter of the story.

Because this is a book made from other books, I also need to offer my deepest thanks to those who came before us. Thank you to Laurel Reuter for her intellectual generosity, her courage, and her willingness to let us excerpt from the outstanding collection of flood books published by the North Dakota Museum of Art. We would not remember the same without all of your hard work. This thanks also must go to Kim Porter, Robin Silverman, and Eliot Glassheim. My admiration, even more than my thanks, also goes to the people of Grand Forks, East Grand Forks, and the Red River Valley. It is no overstatement to say that we wouldn't be here without you.

The new contributors to this book, Janet Rex, Lee Murdock, Leon Osborne, Alice Fothergill, Mike Jacobs, Sherry O'Donnell, Mayor Michael Brown and Josh Roiland also deserve great thanks, because these thanks are all the payment I could offer them. Thank you also to Mayor Lynn Stauss, Gordon Iseminger, Ken Vein, Eliot Glassheim, and Willard Brunelle for graciously speaking with me, my editors, and my contributors.

This book also required the unflagging support of the UND English department. Thank you to the Crystal Alberts and her class for transcribing the 911 calls, to Kim Donehower for approving the idea of the class despite its unorthodox requirements, to Chris Basgier for pointing students towards the class, to Eric Wolfe for his constant defense of the English department, and to Kristin Ellwanger and Cheryl Misialek for keeping things running smoother than could be expected during a tumultuous year.

Thanks also to Emily Montgomery and Mackenzie Teepen at *The Beat* for supporting my schemes. Thank you Mellissa Gjellstadt for talking to my students about the public uses of the humanities, and Bret Weber, Peter Johnson, Susie Caraher, and Pete Haga in the Grand Forks Mayor's office for helping to make our work more public.

I also must stress that this book would not have been possible without the intellectual and aesthetic support of Bill Caraher. Thank you for living up to your promises of deep collaboration, and for all of your work shaping, defending, and designing this book.

Thanks also to my parents, Holly and Mick, for showing me why it is worth preserving the past.

And, obvs, thanks to Sheila, for making me into we.

www.ingramcontent.com/pod-product-compliance
Lightning Source LLC
Chambersburg PA
CBHW061427040426
42450CB00007B/929